About the Marine Sanctuaries Conservation Series

The Office of National Marine Sanctuaries, part of the National Oceanic and Atmospheric Administration, serves as the trustee for a system of 14 marine protected areas encompassing more than 170,000 square miles of ocean and Great Lakes waters. The 13 national marine sanctuaries and one marine national monument within the National Marine Sanctuary System represent areas of America's ocean and Great Lakes environment that are of special national significance. Within their waters, giant humpback whales breed and calve their young, coral colonies flourish, and shipwrecks tell stories of our maritime history. Habitats include beautiful coral reefs, lush kelp forests, whale migrations corridors, spectacular deep-sea canyons, and underwater archaeological sites. These special places also provide homes to thousands of unique or endangered species and are important to America's cultural heritage. Sites range in size from one square mile to almost 140,000 square miles and serve as natural classrooms, cherished recreational spots, and are home to valuable commercial industries.

Because of considerable differences in settings, resources, and threats, each marine sanctuary has a tailored management plan. Conservation, education, research, monitoring and enforcement programs vary accordingly. The integration of these programs is fundamental to marine protected area management. The Marine Sanctuaries Conservation Series reflects and supports this integration by providing a forum for publication and discussion of the complex issues currently facing the sanctuary system. Topics of published reports vary substantially and may include descriptions of educational programs, discussions on resource management issues, and results of scientific research and monitoring projects. The series facilitates integration of natural sciences, socioeconomic and cultural sciences, education, and policy development to accomplish the diverse needs of NOAA's resource protection mandate.

Knowledge, Attitudes and Perceptions of Management Strategies and Regulations of the Gray's Reef National Marine Sanctuary by Users and Non-users of the Sanctuary: Version 2

Vernon R. Leeworthy[1]

1. NOAA, National Ocean Service, Office of National Marine Sanctuaries

U.S. Department of Commerce
Rebecca Blank, Acting Secretary

National Oceanic and Atmospheric Administration
Kathryn Sullivan, Ph.D.
Acting Under Secretary of Commerce for Oceans and Atmosphere

National Ocean Service
Holly Bamford, Ph.D.,Assistant Administrator

Office of National Marine Sanctuaries
Daniel J. Basta, Director

Silver Spring, Maryland
April 2013

DISCLAIMER

Report content does not necessarily reflect the views and policies of the Office of National Marine Sanctuaries or the National Oceanic and Atmospheric Administration, nor does the mention of trade names or commercial products constitute endorsement or recommendation for use.

REPORT AVAILABILITY

Electronic copies of this report may be downloaded from the Office of National Marine Sanctuaries web site at www.sanctuaries.nos.noaa.gov. Hard copies may be available from the following address:

> National Oceanic and Atmospheric Administration
> Office of National Marine Sanctuaries
> SSMC4, N/NMS1
> 1305 East-West Highway
> Silver Spring, MD 20910

COVER

Diver, Atlantic spadefish and "live bottom" at Gray's Reef. Photo by Greg McFall.

SUGGESTED CITATION

Leeworthy, V.R. 2013. Knowledge, Attitudes and Perceptions of Management Strategies and Regulations of the Gray's Reef National Marine Sanctuaries by Users and Non-users of the Sanctuary: Version 2. Marine Sanctuaries Conservation Series ONMS-13-04. U.S. Department of Commerce, National Oceanic and Atmospheric Administration, Office of National Marine Sanctuaries, Silver Spring, MD. 76 pp.

CONTACT

Dr. Vernon R. (Bob) Leeworthy
Chief Economist
Office of National Marine Sanctuaries
1305 East West Highway, SSMC4, 11th floor
Silver Spring, MD 20910
Telephone: (301) 713-7261
Fax: (301) 713-0404
E-mail: Bob.Leeworthy@noaa.gov

Acknowledgements

I would first like to acknowledge the special assistance of interns Lindsay Williamson and Hope Carter of Georgia Southern University. Under the guidance of Dr. John Peden, Assistant Professor, Recreation & Tourism Management, Lindsay and Hope conducted the Version 1 mail surveys of users and non-users of Gray's Reef and entered the returned questionnaires in databases. I would also like to thank Gail Oberg of the Skidaway Institute of Oceanography for her support throughout the long process to get the surveys going. For the Version 2 survey we would like to thank Grant Shillington of Savannah Country Day School who volunteered his time is undertaking the role if getting the mail surveys out and entering the data into databases. We would also like to thank Jody Patterson for her assistance is both recruiting Grant Shillington as a volunteer and providing supervision.

An extra special thank you goes to Becky Shortland for weighing in to complete the data entry and data documentation when the student interns had to get back to school. Becky also undertook the task of doing all the page-layout work for Version 2 of the report.

Superintendent of Gray's Reef, George Sedberry, did a great job of reviewing and editing the report. In addition, his Foreword to the report lays out the motivation for this study. I would also like to thank Greg McFall for the nice photo of Gray's Reef on the cover. I would also like to thank Manoj Shivlani and Christy Loper for their peer review comments and suggestions. Of course any errors in substance or content of the report are solely the responsibility of the author.

FOREWORD

As part of the 2006 management plan for Gray's Reef National Marine Sanctuary, NOAA committed to increasing the public knowledge of the Sanctuary environment to further develop an informed constituency, with the goal to increase awareness, understanding and stewardship of the sanctuary. A challenge noted in the 2006 plan was that of increasing broad public awareness of Gray's Reef as a national treasure and a local natural resource. It was noted such public awareness programs should be developed and implemented with an assessment component to gauge their effectiveness. To address this, the sanctuary proposed a survey be conducted of public perceptions among private boaters to develop a baseline indicator of their knowledge of the sanctuary, its programs, and related coastal ocean issues. The 2006 management plan also proposed a survey be conducted among a broader segment of the general public. Results of the first surveys were reported in March 2012.

The results reported herein incorporate a second survey to users. Both reports implemented as a result of the 2006 management plan are reported herein, and can now be used to develop and improve our communications strategy, and to evaluate the effectiveness of our public education and outreach programs. The findings in this report and the 2012 report survey and results described in this report address those needs outlined in 2006, and provide a background for going forward as we revise the 2006 plan for future management of the sanctuary.

George Sedberry
Superintendent
Gray's Reef National Marine Sanctuary

ABSTRACT

This research is part of the Socioeconomic Research & Monitoring Program for the NOAA Office of National Marine Sanctuaries. In 2010, a baseline study of users and non-users of Gray's Reef National Marine Sanctuary (GRNMS) was initiated. Mail surveys were designed in 2010 and implemented in 2011 and 2012.

The study provides baseline data on the knowledge, attitudes and perceptions of users and non-users of GRNMS in regard to management strategies and regulations. It also provides information on socioeconomic/demographic profiles, activity participation and use of coastal and ocean waters off the Georgia coast both inside and outside GRNMS. The surveys collected data on sources of public information on GRNMS used and the amount of trust in sources used, familiarity with GRNMS rules and regulations, and attitudes about selected management strategies for coastal and ocean resources both inside and outside GRNMS. For users of GRNMS, perceptions of resource conditions were also addressed.

For users and non-users, two versions of the surveys were designed to address all the issues above. Both versions of the survey were implemented for separate samples of non-users of GRNMS in 2011. For users, Version 1 of the survey was implemented in 2011 and Version 2, which obtains information about attitudes on selected management strategies for coastal and ocean resources both inside and outside GRNMS was implemented in 2012.

Previous reports reported the findings from the surveys of users and non-users implemented in 2011 (Leeworthy 2012a and Leeworthy 2012b), while this report provides the results of version 2 of the surveys of users and compares the results of version 2 of the survey for users and non-users which focused on various management strategies in coastal and ocean areas.

Key Findings

Users of GRNMS

- The only significant differences between respondents to versions 1 and 2 of the survey were in:

    ◦ Sources of information used - version 2 respondents used Georgia Sea Grant and the International Game and Fish Association (IGFA) more than version 1 respondents did;

    ◦ Level of trust in sources of information used - version 2 respondents had less trust in information from GRNMS staff and from the GRNMS web site.

- Support for selected management strategies for coastal and ocean resources off the coast of Georgia inside versus outside GRNMS:

  ○ More than 60% of users did not support the use of marine zoning off the coast of Georgia;

  ○ An overwhelming majority of users showed no support for or were somewhat against marine reserves (no-take areas) off Georgia outside GRNMS (78.57%) and inside GRNMS (71.43%);

  ○ An overwhelming majority of users showed no support at all for or were somewhat against research-only areas in coastal and ocean waters off Georgia outside GRNMS (78.05%) and inside GRNMS (78.05%);

  ○ Only a little over one-third of users strongly supported or somewhat supported the multi-species approach to fishery management;

  ○ Over 38% showed no support for or were somewhat against the multi-species approach to fishery management;

  ○ A majority of users would not support an ecosystem-based approach to management of coastal and ocean resources with more than 54% with either no support at all for or somewhat against;

  ○ Only 20.46% strongly supported or somewhat supported an ecosystem-based approach to management of coastal and ocean resources.

- Concern about the health of ocean areas in and around Georgia outside GRNMS:

  ○ An overwhelming majority of users were somewhat concerned to extremely concerned about:

    -Coral reef health or other live bottom habitat (73.81%);
    -Marine animal's health (71.43%);
    -Habitat loss from coastal development (76.19%)
    -Pollution-contaminants such as mercury, PCBs, sewage, pesticides (83.33%).

  ○ A majority was somewhat concerned to extremely concerned about:

    -Overfishing (56.10%);
    -Dredging/offshore dredge disposal (54.76%);
    -Mining of minerals (50%).

- Less than a majority were somewhat concerned to extremely concerned about the three issues related to climate change:

  -Ocean acidification (42.85%);
  -Climate change (33.33%);
  -Sea level rise (30.95%).

- Concern about the health of ocean areas in GRNMS:

  - An overwhelming majority of users were somewhat concerned to extremely concerned about:

    -Coral reef health or other live bottom habitat (76.19%);
    -Marine animal's health (61.91%);
    -Dredging/offshore dredge disposal (60.47%);
    -Habitat loss from coastal development (62.79%);
    -Pollution-contaminants such as mercury, PCBs, sewage, pesticides (81.40%).

  - A majority of users were somewhat concerned to extremely concerned about:

    -Overfishing (50%);
    -Mining of minerals (51.17%).

  - As with the areas outside GRNMS, less than a majority were somewhat concerned to extremely concerned about the three items related to climate change:

    -Ocean acidification (47.62%):
    -Climate change (34.15%);
    -Sea level rise (26.19%).

- Support for protections of coastal and ocean resources off the coast of Georgia inside versus outside of GRNMS:

  - About 55% somewhat supported to strongly supported the protection of coastal and ocean resources outside GRNMS;

  - About 63% supported protection of ocean resources inside GRNMS.

- Ways users of GRNMS value ocean and coastal resources/marine environment:

  - An overwhelming majority of users had high values to extremely high values for the support of recreation activities (85.72%).

- A majority of users of GRNMS had high values to extremely high values for the support for education (59.09%).

- Activities or actions users of GRNMS would undertake to ensure that ocean and coastal resources are used sustainably and available for future generations to enjoy:

  - A majority would do some to do the maximum for four of the nine activity/actions;

    -Volunteer time
    -Donate to groups representing recreational fishing intersts
    -Recycle
    -Use less energy

  - The four activities/actions that a majority would do very little or not at all are:

    -Pay higher taxes for resource protection and restoration;
    -Pay higher prices for goods and services due to costs to business in complying with regulations that protect ocean and coastal resources or require restoration of damaged areas;
    -Pay user fees like fishing licenses or diving access fees or additional boat registration fees;
    -Donate to groups representing diving interests.

Statistically significant differences between users and non-users of GRNMS

- Support for selected management strategies for coastal and ocean resources off the coast of Georgia inside versus outside GRNMS:

  - Use of marine zoning: Non-users were much more supportive of the use of marine zoning in the ocean and coastal areas off the coast of Georgia than users. Non-users overwhelmingly supported the approach with about 76% responding yes, while users were overwhelmingly against with more than 60% responding no.

  - Use of marine reserves (no-take areas): Non-users were much more supportive of the use of marine reserves both outside and inside GRNMS than users. About 82% of non-users either strongly supported or somewhat supported marine reserves outside GRNMS. About 81% either strongly supported or somewhat supported marine reserves inside

GRNMS. In stark contrast, 78.57% of users either had no support at all or were somewhat against marine reserves both outside and inside of GRNMS.

- ◦ Research-only areas: As with all zoning strategies, non-users were much more supportive of the use of research-only areas both outside and inside GRNMS than users. More than 80% of non-users either strongly supported or somewhat supported both the use of research-only areas outside and inside GRNMS. Again in stark contrast, more than 78% of users either had no support at all or were somewhat against the use of research-only areas both outside and inside GRNMS.

- ◦ Multi-species fishery management: Non-users were more supportive of this approach to fishery management than users. But neither group had a majority supporting this approach. A majority of non-users were neutral (52.86%) and a plurality (38.63%) of users either had no support at all or were somewhat against this approach. More than 39% of non-users either strongly supported or somewhat supported this approach, while 34% of users either strongly supported or somewhat supported this approach.

- ◦ Ecosystem-based approach to management of coastal and ocean resources: Again, non-users were more supportive of this approach than users. About 60% of non-users either strongly supported or somewhat supported this approach, while only about 20% of users either strongly supported or somewhat supported this approach. A majority of users (54.55%) either had no support at all or were somewhat against this approach.

- • Support for protections of coastal and ocean resources off the coast of Georgia inside versus outside of GRNMS:

  - ◦ Non-users had significantly more support for protection of resources both outside and inside GRNMS;

  - ◦ More than 94% of non-users either strongly or somewhat supported protection outside GRNMS, while about 55% of users either strongly supported or somewhat supported protection outside GRNMS.

  - ◦ Similarly, about 89% of non-users either strongly supported or somewhat supported protections inside GRNMS, while about 63% of users either strongly supported or somewhat supported protections inside GRNMS.

- Concern about the health of ocean areas in and around Georgia outside of GRNMS:

  - There were statistically significant differences between users and non-users for 12 of the 14 issues; mining of minerals and habitat loss from coastal development were the two issues where there was no statistically significant difference between users and non-users;

  - Both users and non-users had relatively high concern for habitat loss from coastal development and a moderate concern for mining of minerals.

  - Non-users were more concerned than users for the other 12 issues.

- Concern about the health of ocean areas inside GRNMS:

  - There were statistically significant differences between users and non-users for 13 of the 14 issues;

  - Both users and non-users were only moderately concerned with mining of minerals, the only issue where there was no statistically significant difference;

  - As with the concerns outside GRNMS, non-users of GRNMS were more concerned with all the other issues inside GRNMS than users.

- Ways users versus non-users value ocean and coastal resources/marine environment:

  - Non-users had higher values for all 10 of the uses of GRNMS than users except for recreation activities;

  - The differences in levels of values between users and non-users were statistically significant for all 10 uses.

Activities or actions users versus non-users of GRNMS would undertake to ensure that ocean and coastal resources are used sustainably and are available for future generations to enjoy:

- A majority of both users and non-users would volunteer some or to the maximum (67.5% for users and 55.5% for non-users);

- A majority of both users and non-users would not pay higher taxes or would pay very little (72% for users and about 60% for non-users);

- A majority of users (56.82%) would not do or would do very little in paying higher prices as a result of regulations, while a majority of non-users (58.65%) were neutral on this issue;

- A majority of users (about 66%) were opposed to paying higher user fees compared to about 19% of non-users;

- The differences in willingness to donate to groups representing recreational fishing interests correlates with user participation rates in recreational fishing, with users willing to donate more than non-users;

- Both users and non-users have low participation rates in diving and a majority of both users and non-users would not donate or would donate very little to groups representing diving interests.

- More than 88% of users would do some or the maximum recycling, while about 96% of non-users would do some to do the maximum;

- A majority of both users (77%) and non-users (95%) would also be willing to use less energy;

- A majority of both users and non-users were willing to avoid or boycott certain seafood products, but the differences were not significant.

KEY WORDS

Socioeconomic monitoring, knowledge, attitudes, perceptions, management strategies, regulations, users, non-users, activity participation, resource conditions, and socioeconomic/demographic profiles.

TABLE OF CONTENTS

Table of Contents (continued)

TABLE OF CONTENTS (CONTINUED)

TABLE OF CONTENTS (CONTINUED)

List of Tables

List of Figures

Chapter 2: Users of GRNMS Versions 1 and 2 Pooled

List of Tables

List of Figures

Chapter 3: User and Non-user Comparisons Version 2

List of Tables

List of Figures

Introduction

In 2010, a baseline study of users and non-users of Gray's Reef National Marine Sanctuary (GRNMS) was initiated. Mail surveys were designed in 2010 and implemented in 2011 for users and non-users and again in 2012 for users.

The study provides baseline data on the knowledge, attitudes and perceptions of users and non-users of GRNMS in regard to management strategies and regulations. It also provides information on socioeconomic/demographic profiles, activity participation and use of coastal and ocean waters off the Georgia coast both inside and outside GRNMS.

Surveys

Separate surveys of users and non-users of GRNMS were conducted. Non-users were limited to the people living in households of the State of Georgia. The surveys collected data on sources of public information on GRNMS used and the trust of sources used, familiarity with GRNMS rules and regulations, and attitudes about selected management strategies for coastal and ocean resources both inside and outside GRNMS. For users of GRNMS, perceptions of resource conditions were also addressed.

For users and non-users, two versions of the surveys were designed to address all the issues above. Both versions of the survey were implemented for separate samples of non-users of GRNMS in 2011. For users, Version 1 of the survey was implemented in 2011. Version 2, which obtains information about attitudes on selected management strategies for coastal and ocean resources both inside and outside GRNMS was implemented in 2012. This report provides the results of implementing Version 2 of the User Surveys and provides comparisons with non-users on key coastal and ocean resource management/policy strategies.

Sampling Frames

For users, the sampling frame was from a list of users observed in the GRNMS by the Georgia Department of Natural Resources (GADNR). GADNR randomly either boards boats or writes down the boat registration number of the boats observed in the GRNMS. The random boarding is not related to enforcement actions. For boats boarded, name and address of the boat owner/operator is obtained. GRNMS staff received a list containing 249 names and addresses and/or boat registration numbers. Publicly available boat registration files were used to obtain names and addresses for the boat registration numbers. In subsequent efforts, GADNR added 21 names and addresses that were used for the 2012 Version 2 survey.

For non-users, two samples of households were purchased from INFO USA, Inc., which maintains databases of households for survey research. Each sample consisted of the names and addresses for 500 households and was stratified by coastal and non-coastal counties. Unlike most coastal states, Georgia has very few households living in coastal counties because of the terrain, so we over-sampled coastal counties.

Response Rates

For both users and non-users the Dillman Method (Dillman 1978) of mail surveys was used. A full survey was sent out, and if not returned within two weeks, a post card reminder was sent. If a completed survey was not received after an additional two weeks, a full survey package was sent. In version 1 of the user surveys, there were 249 names and addresses of which 94 were undeliverable resulting in 155 net eligible respondents. Of these respondents 79 or 50.97% responded (Table I.1). In version 2 of the user survey, 21 new names and addresses for users received from GADNR were added to the 155 net eligible respondents obtained from implementing version 1 for a total of 176 net eligible respondents. Of these 176 eligible respondents, 44 completed questionnaires were returned for a response rate of 25% (Table I.1).

For non-users Version 1, 500 surveys were mailed out with 44 undeliverable addresses resulting in 456 net eligible respondents. Of these respondents, 83 or 18.2% responded. For non-users Version 2, 500 surveys were mailed out with 54 undeliverable addresses resulting in 446 net eligible respondents. Of these respondents 60 or 13.45% responded (Table I.1).

Table I.1 *Sample Sizes and Response Rates for the Surveys of Users and Non-users of GRNMS*

	Users Version 1	Users Version 2	Non-users Version 1	Non-users Version 2
Original Mailing List	249	155	500	500
Undeleiverable Addresses	94	0	44	54
New Additions to List Version 2	N/A	21	N/A	N/A
Net Eligible Respondents	155	176	456	446
Responded	79	44	83	60
Net Response Rate	50.97%	25.00%	18.20%	13.45%

Non-response Bias/Sample Weighting

Given the low response rates for non-users, non-response bias analysis was conducted and sample weights created to adjust for non-response bias (For details see Technical Appendix, Leeworthy 2012b). People of Hispanic ethnicity had very low response rates, too low for sample weighting to be effective, so Hispanics are not represented in the non-user surveys. Both version samples respondents were significantly different from the general Georgia population for demographic factors, sex, age, race/ethnicity, educational attainment and household income. However, for non-response bias to exist requires that these factors are also related to the answers to the survey questions. There were only a few questions for which there were any statistically significant different responses by these demographic factors, so there is some non-response bias, but it is small and was adjusted for by sample weighting. Again for details of the non-response bias analysis and the sample weighting see the Technical Appendix (Leeworthy 2012b).

Statistical Tests

When the terms "significant difference" or "statistically significant difference" are used, it means that formal statistical tests were conducted. For categorical variable distributions, Chi-Square tests were conducted. For scores using 5-point Likert scales or continuous variables such as person-days or age of respondents, tests of sample means were conducted using t-tests. Level of significance for all tests was at the .05 level of significance or the 95 percent confidence level.

Background/Other Literature

Several other studies have been done in other National Marine Sanctuaries using the Knowledge, Attitudes and Perceptions framework used here. For the Florida Keys National Marine Sanctuary see Milon et al (1997), Shivlani et al (2008), Suman et al (1999) and Thomas Murray & Associates (2005), and for the Channel Islands National Marine Sanctuary see LaFranchi and Pendleton (2008) and Loper (2008). For the results of version 1 users and versions 1 and 2 for non-users, see Leeworthy (2012 a and 2012b)

Chapter 1: Users of GRNMS Version 2

This chapter includes user profiles for respondents to version 2 of the survey, which include the demographic profiles of users, membership in organizations, boat ownership, activity participation and use, and the factors that determined the choice of using GRNMS. The profiles are followed by users' sources of information used, level of trust in the sources of information used, the perceptions of the status of resource conditions in GRNMS, concerns about the health of coastal and ocean areas inside and outside GRNMS off the Georgia coast, support for protection of coastal and ocean resources inside and outside GRNMS off the Georgia coast, ways users value ocean and coastal resources/marine environment, activities that users would do to ensure the sustainability of coastal and ocean resources, and support for selected policy/management strategies for coastal and ocean resources off the Georgia coast.

User Profiles

Demographics

The survey questionnaire included demographic information on the survey respondent's sex, age, race/ethnicity, educational attainment, employment status, household income, household type, and household size. Users were all white non-Hispanic males with ages ranging from 34 to 76 years (mean 56.59 and median 57) (Table 1.1).

Table 1.1. Sex, Race, and Age of GRNMS Users: Version 2 Survey, 2012

Sex	
Female	0.00%
Male	100.00%
Race	
White	100.00%
Age	
Mean	56.59
Median	57
Minimum	34
Maximum	76

Users had generally high levels of educational attainment with almost 70 percent with "Some College" or above (Figure 1.1). None of the users were unemployed during the 2012 survey period with about 70% employed full-time and more than 25% retired (Figure 1.2). Users also had relatively high household incomes with over half of household incomes over $100,000 (Figure 1.3). Almost 77% of users lived in households without children (Figure 1.4). About 56% lived in households with two people (Figure 1.5) with an average household size of 2.56 (Table 1.2).

4

Users of GRNMS had generally high levels of educational attainment with almost 70 percent with some college or above.

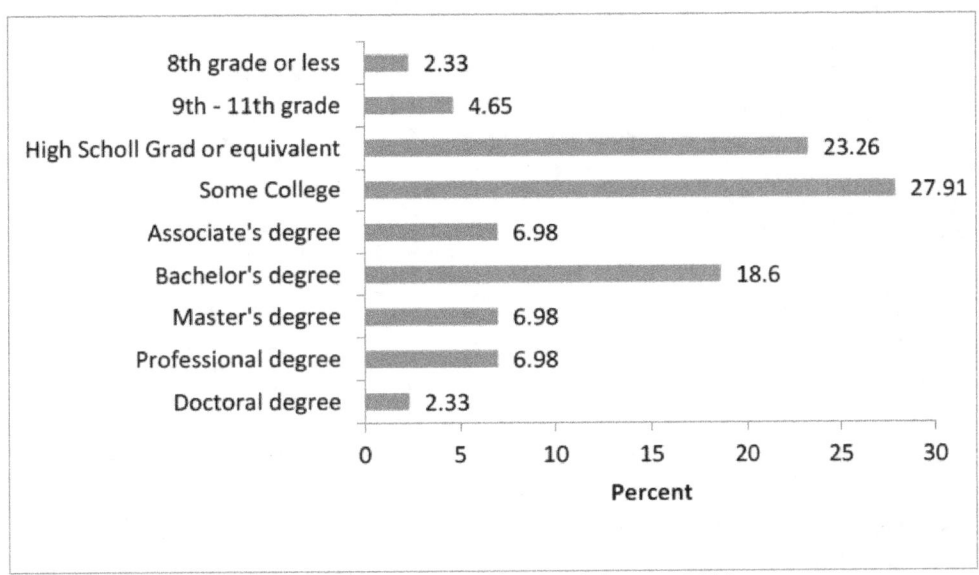

Figure 1.1 *Educational Attainment of Users: Version 2 Survey, 2012*

About 70 percent of GRNMS users were employed full-time with zero unemployed and more than 25 percent retired.

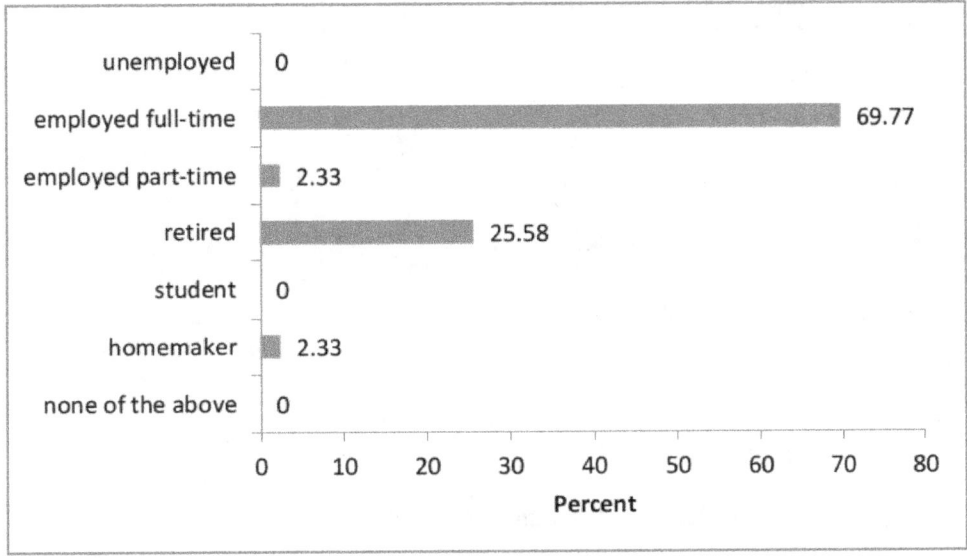

Figure 1.2 *Employment Status of Users: Version 2 Survey, 2012*

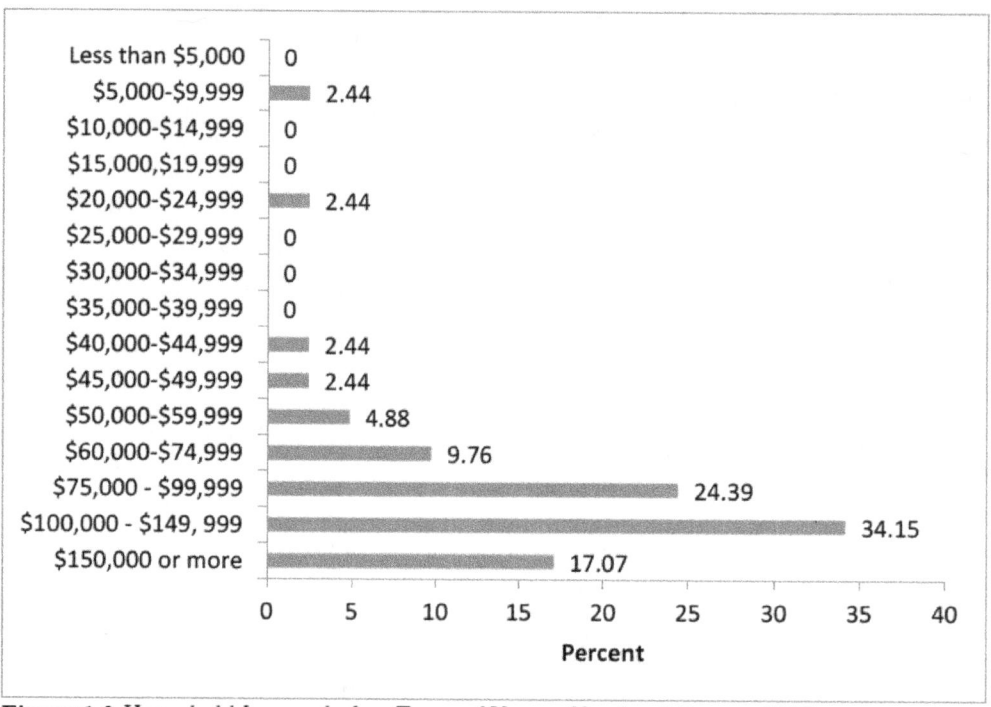

Figure 1.3 *Household Income before Taxes of Users: Version 2 Survey, 2012*

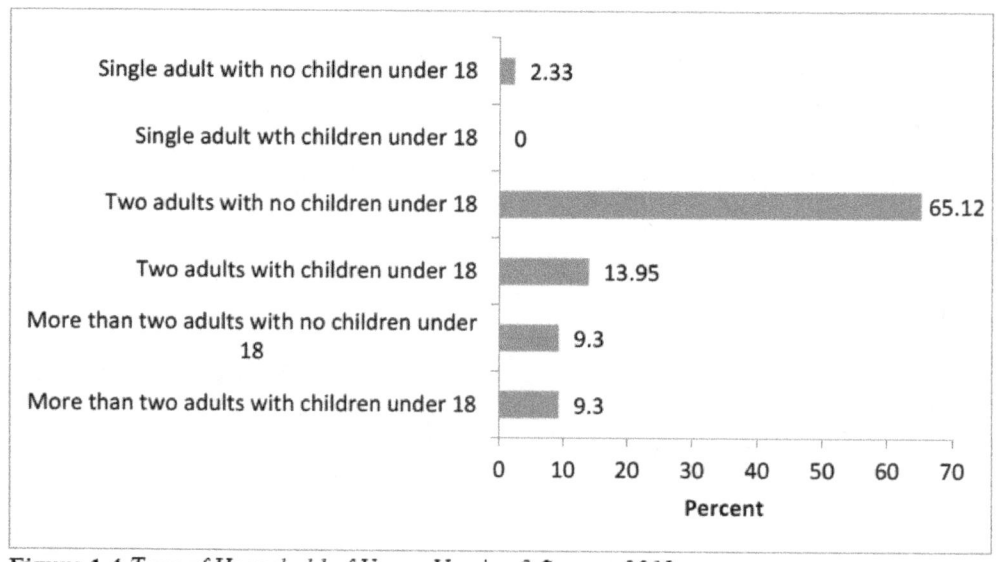

Figure 1.4 *Type of Household of Users: Version 2 Survey, 2012*

Users of GRNMS had household sizes ranging from 1 to 6 persons with a little more than 63 percent in household with two or less persons.

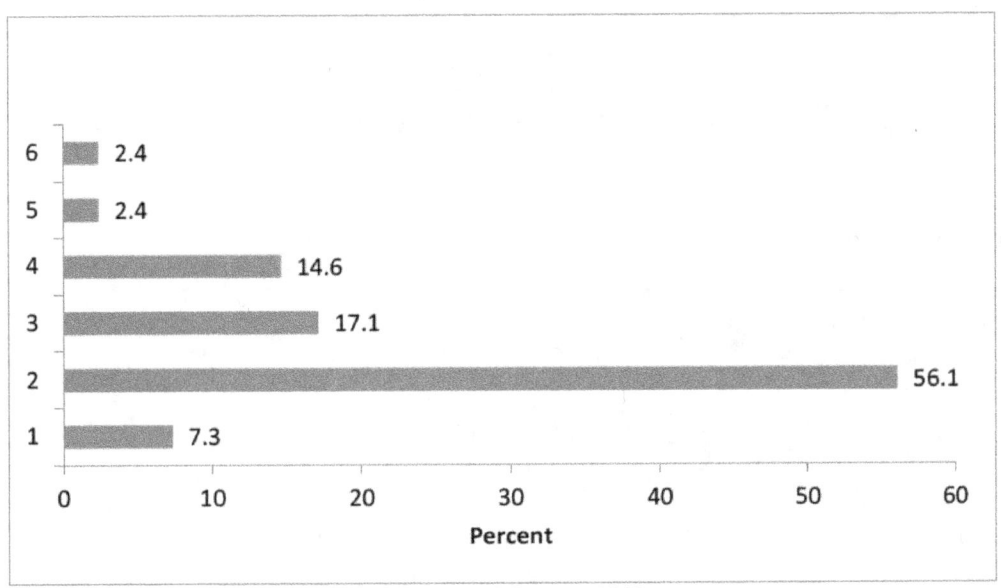

Figure 1.5 *Household Size of Users: Version 2 Survey, 2012*

Table 1. 2. Household Size: Users of GRNMS: Version 2 Survey, 2012

	Mean	Median	Minimum	Maximum
Total Household Size	2.56	2	1	6
Number age 18 or older	2.12	2	1	4
Number under age 18	0.39	0	0	5

Organizational Membership and Boat Ownership

More than half of all users were members of fishing groups, clubs or organizations, while almost 14% were members of chambers of commerce. Also, 6.8% were members of environmental groups (Figure 1.6). More than 97% of users owned a boat ranging from 16 to 35 feet in length (mean 24.07 feet). On average, about three people were aboard the boats when in GRNMS (Table 1.3).

7

More than half of users of GRNMS were members of fishing groups, clubs or organizations, while almost 14 percent were members of chambers of commerce.

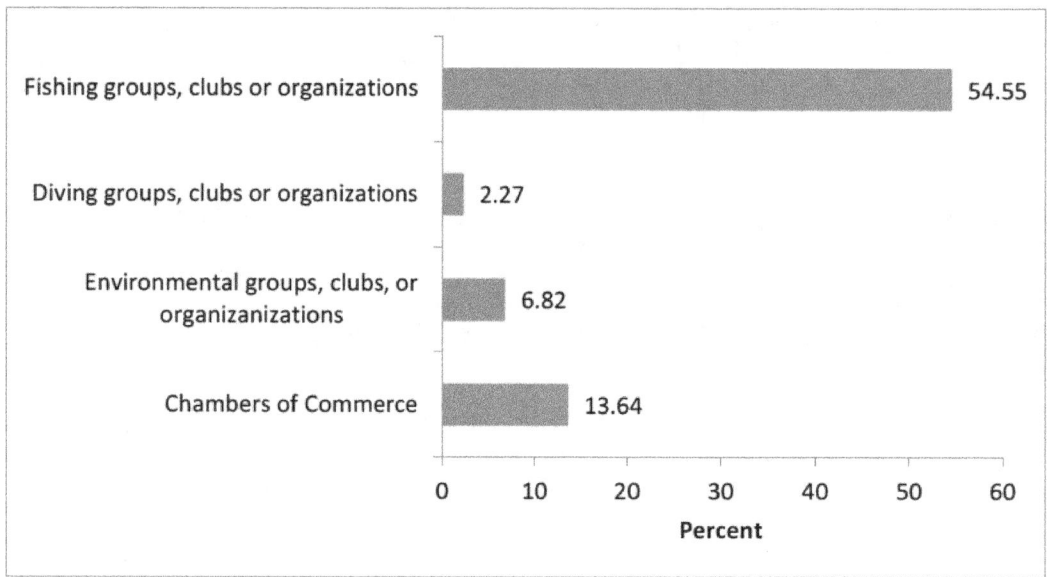

Figure 1.6 *Users' Memberships in Groups, Clubs and Organizations: Version 2 Survey, 2012*

Table 1.3. Boat Ownership and Length of Boat: Users of GRNMS, Version 2, 2012

Do you own a boat? (percent yes)	97.67
Length of Boat Owned (feet)	
Mean	24.07
Median	23
Minimum	16
Maximum	35
Number of People Aboard	
Mean	3.1
Median	3
Minimum	2
Maximum	5

Activity Participation and Use

The survey gathered information on recreation activities that users participated in at GRNMS and in coastal and ocean areas of Georgia outside GRNMS. Activities were classified as those that take place in GRNMS and those that do not take place in GRNMS, but do take place in coastal and ocean areas of Georgia outside GRNMS.

Participation in activities that take place in GRNMS - The survey asked about participation in "recreational bottom fishing", "recreational fishing – trolling or drifting in mid or top water", "recreational spear fishing – with power heads", "recreational spear fishing-without power heads", "SCUBA diving where nothing is taken", "SCUBA diving where something is taken or harvested", "whale watching or other wildlife viewing activities" and "sailing". These activities were then classified into "consumptive" and "nonconsumptive" activities. Figure 1.7 summarizes the results.

Users of GRNMS had higher participation rates in consumptive activities than in nonconsumptive activities in the coastal and ocean waters off Georgia, including GRNMS. About 93% participated in fishing in GRNMS and in the coastal and ocean waters of Georgia outside GRNMS. Even though spear fishing is prohibited in GRNMS, more than 6% of survey respondents said they participated in spear fishing in GRNMS, while more than 13% said they did it in coastal and ocean areas of Georgia outside GRNMS. A little more than 11% participated in SCUBA diving in GRNMS, while almost 18% participated in SCUBA diving in the coastal and ocean waters of Georgia outside GRNMS.

For activities that are known to occur in GRNMS, users of GRNMS had higher participation rates in consumptive activities than nonconsumptive activities in the coastal and ocean waters off Georgia, with 93 percent participating in fishing in either GRNMS or coastal and ocean waters outside GRNMS off the Georgia coast.

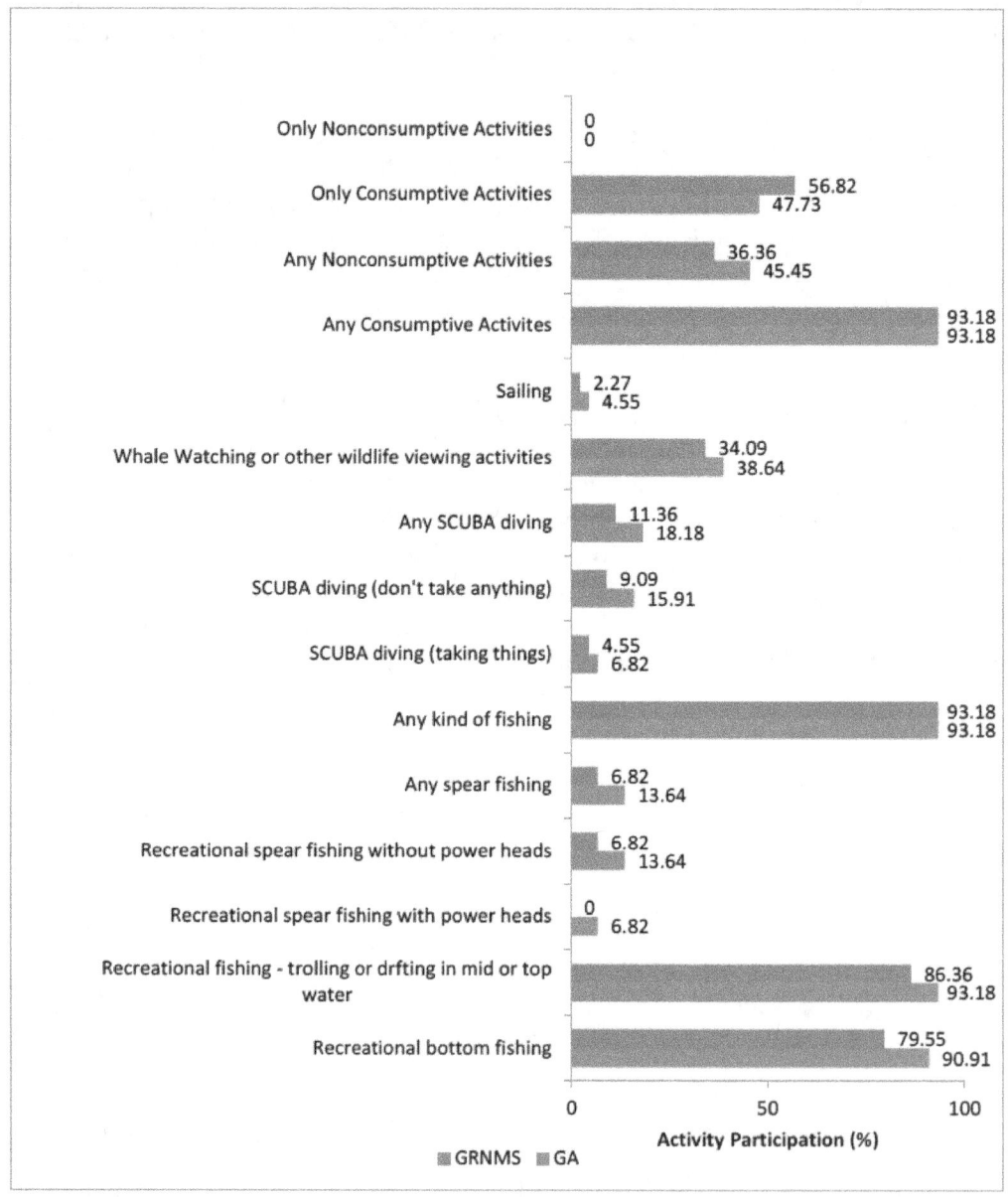

Figure 1.7 *Users' Activity Participation in GA and GRNMS: Version 2 Survey, 2012*

Participation in activities that don't take place in GRNMS - The survey asked about participation in "beach activities", "surfing", "windsurfing or kite boarding", "personal watercraft use (jet skis, wave runners, etc.)", and "shorebird watching". Users of GRNMS had the highest participation in "beach activities" with 81.82% and "shorebird watching" with 34.09%. More than 13% participated in 'personal watercraft use", while more than 11% participated in surfing and "windsurfing or kite boarding" (Figure 1.8).

> For selected activities that don't occur in GRNMS, users of GRNMS had the highest participation in beach and shorebird watching activities in the coastal and ocean waters off Georgia outside GRNMS.

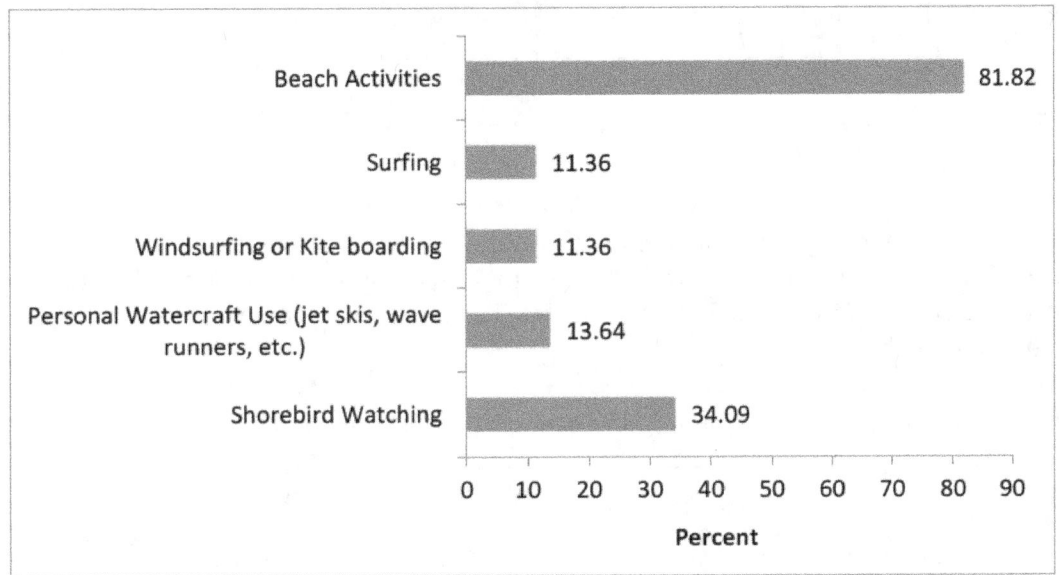

Figure 1.8 *Uses' Activity Participation in Georgia for Selected Activities: Version 2 Survey, 2012*

Person-days of Use by Activity

Intensity of use was measured as annual person-days of use where a person-day is equal to one person doing an activity for a whole day or any part of a day. Survey respondents were asked about their use for the activities that take place in GRNMS and how many person-days were in GRNMS versus how many person-days were in coastal and ocean waters of Georgia outside GRNMS. Results were summarized as the mean number of person-days for "all users", which includes those that did zero days of an activity, and "participants only", which includes only those that did at least one day of an activity (Table 1.4).

Outside GRNMS, users had the highest mean person-days of activity in "recreational bottom fishing" at 29.14 person-days in 2011, while "recreational fishing-trolling or drifting in mid or top water" was second with 21.95 person-days. This difference was statistically significant (Table 1.4).

Table 1.4. Person-days of Activity Participation in GA: Users of GRNMS, Version 2, 2012

Activity	All Users[1] GA (mean)	Participants Only GA (mean)
Recreational bottom fishing	29.14	32.12
Recreational fishing - trolling or drfting in mid or top water	21.95	23.64
Recreational spear fishing with power heads	0.09	*
Recreational spear fishing without power heads	0.22	*
SCUBA diving (taking things)	0.14	*
SCUBA diving (don't take things)	0.52	*
Whale watching or other wildlife viewing activities	2.20	6.77

1. All Users includes people who did not do the activity, so they have zero days of use.
* sample size too small

Inside GRNMS, users had the highest mean person-days of activity in "recreational bottom fishing" with 13.45 person-days for 2011, while "recreational fishing – trolling or drifting in mid or top water" 'was close behind with 10.38 person-days. The difference, however, is not statistically significant (Table 1.5).

Table 1.5. Person-days of Activity Participation in GRNMS: Users of GRNMS, Version 2, 2012

Activity	All Users[1] GRNMS (mean)	Participants Only GRNMS (mean)
Recreational bottom fishing	13.45	17.12
Recreational fishing - trolling or drifting in mid or top water	10.38	12.11
Recreational spear fishing with power heads	0.00	*
Recreational spear fishing without power heads	0.12	*
SCUBA diving (taking things)	0.14	*
SCUBA diving (don't take things)	0.23	*
Whale watching or other wildlife viewing activities	1.75	6.36

1. All Users includes people who did not do the activity, so they have zero days of use.
* sample size too small

Participation in Fishing Tournaments

Survey respondents, who fished, were asked if they participated in fishing tournaments. About 49% participated in fishing tournaments (Figure 1.9).

About 49 percent of Users of GRNMS participate in fishing tournaments

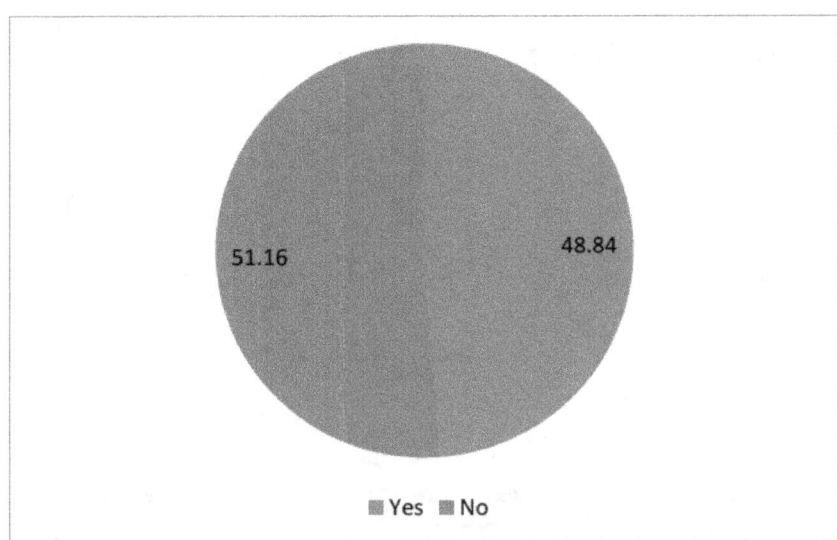

Figure 1.9.*User's Participation in Fishing Tournaments: Version 2 Survey, 2012*

Factors Influencing the Choice of Going to GRNMS for Activities

Survey respondents were asked for the factors that influenced their choices when deciding to go to GRNMS for their activities. For each factor they were asked to respond either "Yes", "Somewhat", or "Not at All". "Fish species preference" and "sea conditions" had the highest proportions of users who said "Yes" with 78.57%. This was followed by "seasonal patterns" (69.23%) and "weather" (66.67%). Even though about 95% fish in GRNMS, only 57.52% said "Yes" to "better fishing" (Table 1.6).

Table 1.6. Factors Influencing Choice of Going to GRNMS for Activities: Users of
           GRNMS Version 2 Survey, 2012

Factor	Yes (%)	Somewhat (%)	Not at All (%)
Weather	66.67	30.95	2.38
Fish species preference	78.57	16.67	4.76
Time of Day	57.89	28.95	13.16
Seasonal patterns	69.23	30.77	0.00
Word of mouth/radio talk	35.14	43.24	21.62
Boat Captain's choice	55.88	8.82	35.29
Sea conditions	78.57	19.05	2.38
Distance to GRNMS	60.00	25.00	15.00
Better fishing	57.50	40.00	2.50
Better diving for things to see	11.54	7.69	80.77

Knowledge

The survey addressed four topics on knowledge: 1) sources of information used, 2) level of trust of information sources used, 3) how users prefer to receive information about GRNMS and 4) familiarity with GRNMS regulations. The "Don't Know" responses to the attitudes and perceptions questions also provide indirect information about user's knowledge.

Sources of Information Used

The survey asked about 22 known possible sources of information and provided for "other" sources responses. The most used sources of information included the "Georgia Department of Natural Resources" (67.44%), "Marinas" (65.67%), "Word of mouth" (62.79%) "Internet" (60.47%), "Fishing magazines/newsletters" (55.81%), "Newspapers" (53.49%), "GRNMS web site" (51.16%), "NOAA's National Marine Fisheries Service" (46.51%) and the "Southern Kingfish Association" (46.51%). Only 16.28% had used "social media (Twitter, You Tube, Facebook, etc.). The full results are summarized in Table 1.7.

14

Table 1.7. Sources of Information Used about GRNMS: Users of GRNMS, Version 2, 2012

Source	Used (% Yes)
Grays Reef National Marine Sanctuary Sanctuary Advisory Council	23.26
Grays Reef National Marine Sanctuary Staff	23.26
Grays Reef National Marine Sanctuary Web site	51.16
NOAA's National Marine Fisheries Service	46.51
Atlantic States Marine Fisheries Commission	18.60
South Atlantic Fishery Management Council	18.60
Georgia Department of Natural Resources	67.44
Georgia Sea Grant	11.63
Coastal Conservation Association of Georgia (CCAGA)	25.58
Recreational Fishing Alliance (RFA)	34.88
American Sportfishing Association (ASA)	25.58
National Coalition for Marine Conservation (NCMC)	9.30
International Game and Fish Association (IGFA)	32.56
Southern Kingfish Association (SKA)	46.51
Fishing Magazines/Newsletters	55.81
SCUBA diving magazines/Newsletters	23.26
Newspapers	53.49
Radio	27.91
Television	46.51
Internet	60.47
Social Media (Twitter, You Tube, Facebook, etc.)	16.28
Word of mouth	62.79
Marinas	65.67
Other Anglers	16.67
Other Divers	33.33

Level of Trust of Information Sources Used

For sources of information used, respondents were asked for their level of trust of the information scored on a five-point Likert scale where 1=No Trust at All and 5=Completely Trust. For the sources that were used the most, the "Georgia Department of Natural Resources" had the highest level of trust with 65.39% trusting it very much or completely trusted. The "Fishing magazines/newsletters" followed with 65.22% trusting it very much or completely trusted and "GRNMS web site" with 52.38% trusting it very much or completely trusted. Although the "Internet" and "Word of mouth" were highly used sources of information, only 24% trusted very much or completely trusted the "Internet", while 44% trusted very much or completely trusted "Word of mouth" (Table 1.8).

Table 1.8. Level of Trust of Information Sources Used: Users of GRNMS Version 2 Survey, 2012

Source	No Trust\ At All	Very Little Trust	Neutral	Trust Very Much	Completely Trust
Grays Reef National Marine Sanctuary Advisory Council	30.00	0.00	10.00	60.00	0.00
Grays Reef National Marine Sanctuary Staff	30.00	0.00	10.00	50.00	10.00
Grays Reef National Marine Sanctuary Web site	4.76	19.05	23.81	47.62	4.76
NOOA's National Marine Fisheries Service	21.05	5.26	26.32	36.84	10.53
Atlantic States Marine Fisheries Commission	25.00	50.00	0.00	25.00	0.00
South Atlantic Fishery Management Council	25.00	37.50	0.00	37.50	0.00
Georgia Department of Natural Resources	3.85	11.54	19.23	42.31	23.08
Georgia Sea Grant	20.00	0.00	60.00	20.00	0.00
Coastal Conservation Association of Georgia (CCAGA)	0.00	0.00	0.00	45.45	54.55
Recreational Fishing Alliance (RFA)	0.00	0.00	7.14	64.29	28.57
American Sportfishing Association (ASA)	0.00	0.00	10.00	60.00	30.00
National Coalition for Marine Conservation (NCMC)	0.00	0.00	50.00	50.00	0.00
International Game and Fish Association (IGFA)	0.00	0.00	21.43	57.14	21.43
Southern Kingfish Association (SKA)	0.00	5.00	5.00	55.00	35.00
Fishing Magazines/Newsletters	0.00	4.35	30.43	65.22	0.00
SCUBA diving magazines/Newsletters	0.00	0.00	37.50	62.50	0.00
Newspapers	0.00	4.76	66.67	23.81	4.76
Radio	0.00	0.00	81.82	9.09	9.09
Television	0.00	10.53	57.89	26.32	5.26
Internet	0.00	4.00	72.00	20.00	4.00
Social Media (Twitter, You Tube, Facebook, etc.)	0.00	14.29	71.43	14.29	0.00
Word of mouth	0.00	8.00	48.00	32.00	12.00

How Users Would Like to Receive Information about GRNMS

Backing up the sources of information used and the level of trust on the sources used, the "GRNMS web site" was chosen as the most preferred way users would like to receive information about GRNMS at 47.73%. A "Newsletter delivered by the U.S. Postal Service" was equally preferred to the "GRNMS web site" (47.73%) closely followed by "E-mail list serve" (45.45%). A "Telephone call from staff" was the least preferred at 13.64% (Figure 1.10).

Most users of GRNMS would prefer to receive information about GRNMS via either the GRNMS web site, newsletter delivered to their home via the U.S. Postal Service, or E-mail list serve.

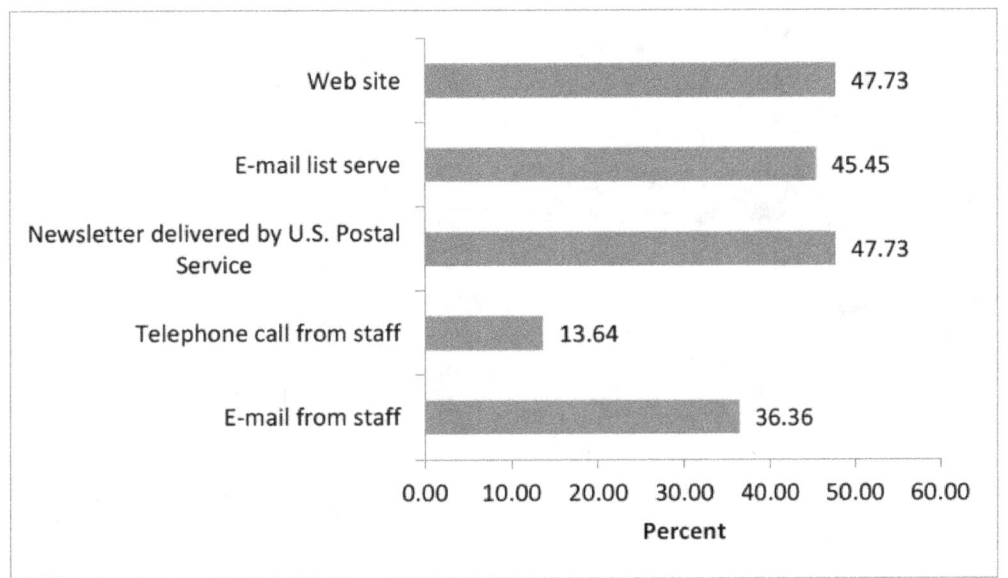

Figure 1.10 *How Users would like to receive information about GRNMS: Version 2 Survey, 2012*

Familiarity with GRNMS Regulations

Survey respondents were also asked for a self-evaluation of their familiarity with the regulations of GRNMS. More than 61% of users said they were "Somewhat familiar" with the regulations and more than 36% said they were "Very familiar" with the regulations. Only 2.27% said they were not at all familiar with the regulations (Figure 1.11).

17

Over 97 percent of users of GRNMS were familiar with GRNMS rules and regulations.

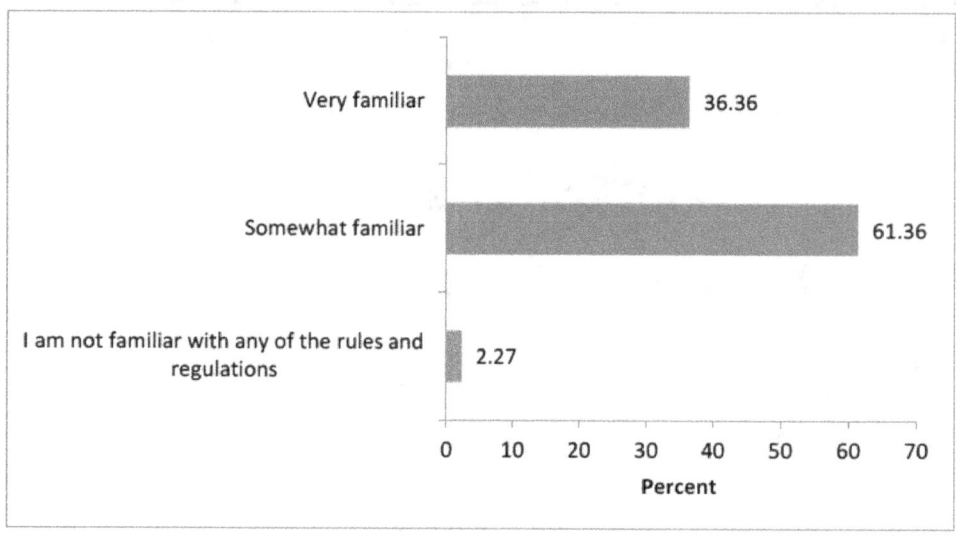

Figure 1.11 *User's Familiarity with GRNMS Rules and Regulations: Version 2 Survey, 2012*

Perceptions

The survey asked users for their perceptions of conditions of 11 resources in GRNMS. Ratings of conditions were asked using a five-point Likert scale with 1=getting a lot better, 2=getting somewhat better, 3=same, 4=getting somewhat worse, and 5=getting a lot worse. A "Don't Know" response was also allowed. A high proportion of users responded that they "Don't Know" for all 11 resources. For all resources, except "Invasive species" a higher proportion of users thought conditions were getting somewhat to a lot better than those who thought conditions were getting somewhat to a lot worse (Table 1.9).

Table 1.9. Perceptions of Conditions of Resources in GRNMS: Users of GRNMS Version 2 Survey, 2012

Resource	Getting a Lot Better	Getting Somewhat Better	Same	Getting Somewhat Worse	Getting a Lot Worse	Don't Know
Live bottom habitat	18.18	25.00	27.27	6.82	2.27	20.45
Other bottom habitat	15.91	25.00	29.55	9.09	0.00	20.45
Fish populations (bottom fish)	18.18	31.82	27.27	6.82	0.00	15.91
Fish populations (pelagic)	18.18	22.73	31.82	15.91	2.27	9.09
Fish populations (diversity or number of	15.91	22.73	43.18	4.55	0.00	13.64
Other Sea life (abundance)	15.91	25.00	36.36	2.27	2.27	18.18
Other Sea life (diversity or number of species)	13.64	22.73	43.18	2.27	0.00	18.18
Water quality	13.64	13.64	40.91	11.36	0.00	20.45
Invasive species (such as lionfish)	2.27	0.00	20.45	22.73	20.45	34.09
Marine debris (plastics, other trash)	9.09	20.45	27.27	20.45	4.55	18.18
Sea based pollution (discharges from boats)	11.36	13.64	47.73	9.09	4.55	13.64

Concern about the Health of Coastal and Ocean Areas

The survey asked respondents about their level of concern on 14 issues regarding the health of ocean and coastal areas. Respondents were first asked about their level of concern for these 14 issues in the coastal and ocean waters in and around Georgia outside GRNMS, then about them inside GRNMS. A five-point Likert scale for level of concern was used with 1=Not concerned at all, 2=Not very concerned, 3=Neutral, 4=Somewhat concerned, and 5=Extremely concerned.

In and Around Georgia outside GRNMS

An overwhelming majority of users were somewhat to extremely concerned about "Coral reef health or other live bottom habitat" (73.81%), "Marine animal's health" (71.43%), "Habitat loss from coastal development (76.19%), and "Pollution-contaminants such as mercury, PCBs, sewage, pesticides" (83.33%). A majority was somewhat to extremely concerned about "Overfishing" (56.10%), "Dredging/Offshore dredge disposal" (54.76%), and "Mining of Minerals" (50%). Less than a majority were somewhat to extremely concerned about the three issues related to climate change "Ocean Acidification" (42.85%), "Climate Change" (33.33%), and "Sea level rise" (30.95%). The full results are summarized in Table 1.10.

Table 1.10. Concern about the Health of Coastal & Ocean Areas in and around Georgia Outside of GRNMS: Users of GRNMS Version 2 Survey, 2012

Issue	Not Concerned at all	Not Very Concerned	Neutral	Somewhat Concerned	Extremely Concerned
a. Ocean acidification	9.52	14.29	33.33	33.33	9.52
b. Climate change	23.81	16.67	26.19	30.95	2.38
c. Sea level rise	23.81	19.05	26.19	28.57	2.38
d. Over fishing (catching more than can be replaced)	19.51	9.76	14.63	29.27	26.83
e. Coral reef health or other live bottom habitat	4.76	7.14	14.29	38.10	35.71
f. Marine animal's health	7.14	4.76	16.67	52.38	19.05
g. Shipping (marine transportation)	11.90	21.43	30.95	23.81	11.90
h. Dredging/Offshore dredge disposal	7.14	19.05	19.05	35.71	19.05
i. Beach renourishment	7.14	19.05	35.71	28.57	9.52
j. Energy production (oil & gas)	23.61	21.43	21.43	16.67	16.67
k. Alternative energy production (wind, tidal, and wave)	21.43	23.81	28.57	19.05	7.14
l. Mining of minerals (including sand)	11.90	21.43	16.67	28.57	21.43
m. Habitat loss from coastal development	2.38	16.67	4.76	40.48	35.71
n. Pollution (contaminants such as mercury, PCBs, sewage, pesticides)	2.38	2.38	11.90	28.57	54.76

In GRNMS

An overwhelming majority of users were somewhat to extremely concerned about "Coral reef health or other live bottom habitat" (76.19%), "Marine animal's health" (61.91%), "Dredging/Offshore dredge disposal" (60.47%), "Habitat loss from coastal development" (62.79%), and "Pollution-contaminants such as mercury, PCBs, sewage, pesticides" (81.40%). A majority of users were somewhat to extremely concerned about "Over fishing" (50%) and "Mining of minerals" (51.17%). As with the areas outside GRNMS, less than a majority were somewhat to extremely concerned about the three items related to climate change "Ocean acidification "(47.62%), "Climate change" (34.15%) and "Sea level rise" (26.19%). The full results are summarized in Table 1.11.

Table 1.11. Concern about the Health of Ocean Areas in GRNMS: Users of GRNMS Version 2 Survey, 2012

Issue	Not Concerned at all	Not Very Concerned	Neutral	Somewhat Concerned	Extremely Concerned
a. Ocean acidification	11.90	9.52	30.95	33.33	14.29
b. Climate change	24.39	14.63	26.83	26.83	7.32
c. Sea level rise	26.19	19.05	28.57	21.43	4.76
d. Over fishing (catching more than can be replaced)	28.57	7.14	14.29	28.57	21.43
e. Coral reef health or other live bottom habitat	4.76	7.14	11.90	42.86	33.33
f. Marine animal's health	4.76	7.14	26.19	42.86	19.05
g. Shipping (marine transportation)	7.14	21.43	38.10	19.05	14.29
h. Dredging/Offshore dredge disposal	4.65	18.60	16.28	32.56	27.91
i. Beach renourishment	9.30	18.60	34.88	23.26	13.95
j. Energy production (oil & gas)	23.26	23.26	18.60	11.63	23.26
k. Alternative energy production (wind, tidal, and wave)	20.93	25.58	30.23	11.63	11.63
l. Mining of minerals (including sand)	13.95	18.60	16.28	23.26	27.91
m. Habitat loss from coastal development	2.33	16.28	18.60	30.23	32.56
n. Pollution (contaminants such as mercury, PCBs, sewage, pesticides)	0.00	4.65	13.95	32.56	48.84

Support for Protection of Coastal and Ocean Resources

The survey asked respondents about their level of support for protection of resources outside and inside GRNMS. A five-point Likert scale for support was used with 1=no support at all, 2=somewhat against, 3=neutral, 4=somewhat support, and 5=strongly support. About 55% somewhat to strongly supported the protection of coastal and ocean resources outside GRNMS, while about 63% supported protection of ocean resources inside GRNMS (Table 1.12).

Table 1.12. Support for Protection of Coastal & Ocean Resources in and around Georgia Outside of GRNMS versus Inside GRNMS: Users of GRNMS Version 2 Survey, 2012

	No Support at All	Somewhat Against	Neutral	Somewhat Support	Strongly Support
a. Protection Outside GRNMS	9.52	28.57	7.14	33.33	21.43
b. Protection Inside GRNMS	11.63	16.28	9.3	37.21	25.58

Ways Users of GRNMS Value Coastal and Ocean Resources/Marine Environment

The survey asked respondents for their level of value for 10 uses of coastal and ocean resources. The level of value used was a five-point Likert scale where 1=no value, 2=low value, 3=medium value, 4=high value, and 5=extremely high value. An overwhelming majority of users had high to extremely high value for the "Support of recreation activities" (85.72%). A majority of users of GRNMS had high to extremely high values for "Support for education" (59.09%). The full results are summarized in Table 1.13.

Table 1.13. Ways Users of GRNMS Value Coastal & Ocean Resources/Marine Environment Version 2 Survey, 2012

Good or Service	No Value	Low Value	Medium Value	High Value	Extremely High Value
a. Support for recreation activities	2.38	2.38	9.52	45.24	40.48
b. Seafood purchased at local stores and restaurants	4.65	18.60	27.91	25.58	23.26
c. Seafood purchased at non local stores & restaurants	26.19	26.19	35.71	7.14	4.76
d. Support for Scientific Research	6.82	9.09	40.91	27.27	15.91
e. Support for education	6.82	2.27	31.82	34.09	25.00
f. Supply of mineral resources through mining	29.55	27.27	34.09	6.82	2.27
g. Supply of oil & gas	16.28	9.30	34.88	13.95	25.58
h. Supply of alternative energy (wind, wave, tidal)	15.91	13.64	36.36	18.18	15.91
i. Supply of pharmaceutical products through mining or harvest of resources	20.45	27.27	25.00	18.18	9.09
j. Protection of resources even though I never intend to visit or directly use them	11.36	11.36	34.09	25.00	18.18

Actions Users of GRNMS Would Take to Ensure Sustainability of Coastal and Ocean Resources

The survey asked respondents about the activities or actions they would take to ensure that coastal and ocean resources are used sustainably and available for future generations. Nine activities or actions were presented and a five-point Likert scale was used to score to what extent respondents would undertake each activity or action, where 1=would not do, 2=would do very little, 3=would do some, 4=would do a lot, and 5=would do the maximum. A majority would do some to the maximum for five of the nine activity/actions. The four activities/actions that a majority would do very little or not at all was "Pay higher taxes for resource protection and restoration", "Pay higher prices for goods and services due to costs to business in complying with regulations that protect ocean and coastal resources or require restoration of damaged areas" "Pay user fees like fishing licenses or diving access fees or additional boat registration fees" and "Donate to groups representing diving interests". Very few users participated in diving activities in GRNMS so the low level of willingness to support groups representing diving interests is understandable. The negative reaction to all three issues of higher taxes, prices and user fees - the latter which is a more complicated issue - is quite surprising.

The literature on user fees supports the notion that people are willing to pay user fees for the activities that they participate in (Aukerman 1987, Brown 1992, Fedler and Miles 1989, Kyle et al 2002, Leeworthy 1993, and Winter et al 1999). They do not want to subsidize the activities of others. If general taxes are used to pay to support recreational or other activities or goods and services they don't consume, they generally do not support them. This is what is being picked up by the response to "Pay higher taxes for resource protection and restoration". One can see this more clearly by looking at the response to "Pay higher prices for goods and services due to costs to businesses in complying with regulations that protect ocean and coastal resources or require restoration of areas damaged". In this case, people are paying only for the goods and services they consume through the prices that are passed onto them by suppliers. The full results are summarized in Table 1.14.

Table 1.14. Activities or Actions Users of GRNMS Would Do to ensure that coastal and ocean resources are used sustainably and available for future generations to enjoy: Version 2 Survey 2012

Activity or Action	Would Not Do	Would do Very Little	Would Do Some	Would Do a Lot	Would do the Maximum
a. Volunter time	7.50	25.00	50.00	15.00	2.50
b. Pay higher taxes for resource protection and restoration	46.51	26.58	20.93	2.33	4.65
c. Pay higher prices for goods and services due to costs to businesses in complying with regulations that protect ocean & coastal resources or require restoration of areas damaged	31.82	25.00	25.00	6.82	11.36
d. Pay user fees like fishing licenses or diving access fees or additional boat registration fees	38.64	27.27	27.27	4.55	2.27
e. Donate to groups respresenting recreational fishing interests	11.63	9.30	51.16	20.93	6.98
f. Donate to groups representing diving interests	42.86	19.05	26.19	9.52	2.38
g. Recycle	4.65	6.98	32.56	32.56	23.26
h. Use less energy	6.98	16.28	41.86	16.29	18.60
i. Avoid/boycott certain seafood products	25.00	15.91	29.55	11.36	18.18

Support for Selected Policy/Management Strategies for Coastal and Ocean Resources

The survey addressed three general kinds of controversial policy/management strategies that have been implemented in various places or that are being considered in managing coastal and ocean resources: marine zoning where certain activities are prohibited or restricted, multi-species fishery management where fishery managers must take into account the inter-relationships among species, and ecosystem-based management where all uses and all resources are given consideration in management. For marine zoning, two special forms of zones are addressed: marine reserves or "no take" areas where only non-consumptive activities are allowed, and "research only areas" where only scientific and educational activities are allowed. For these two types of zones, opinions of respondents were also obtained as to what extent of displacement of activities was acceptable.

Marine Zoning

Survey respondents were first asked if they supported the use of marine zoning in coastal and ocean areas. More than 60% of users of GRNMS did not support the use of marine zoning (Figure 1.12).

A little over 60 percent of Users of GRNMS would not support the use of marine zoning in the coastal and ocean waters off the coast of Georgia.

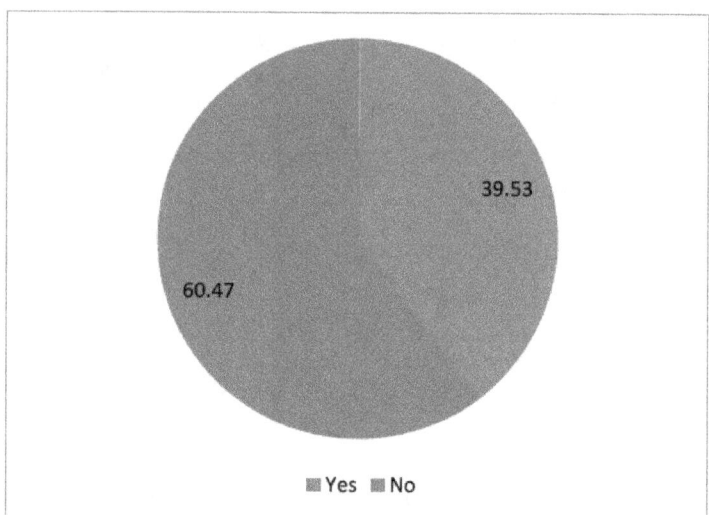

Figure 1.12 Users' Support for Marine Zoning off the Coast of Georgia: Version 2 Survey, 2012

Marine Reserves

Survey respondents were asked for their level of support for marine reserves or "no take" areas in the coastal and ocean waters off Georgia outside GRNMS and inside GRNMS. Level of support was measured using a five-point Likert scale where 1=no support at all, 2=somewhat against, 3=neutral, 4=somewhat support, and 5=strongly support. An overwhelming majority had no support at all or was somewhat against marine reserves in coastal and ocean waters off Georgia outside GRNMS (78.57%) and inside GRNMS (71.43%), with slightly less opposition for marine reserves in GRNMS.

24

An overwhelming majority of Users of GRNMS would not support the creation of marine reserves in the coastal and ocean waters off the coast of Georgia both inside and outside GRNMS with slightly lower support for the marine reserves outside the GRNMS.

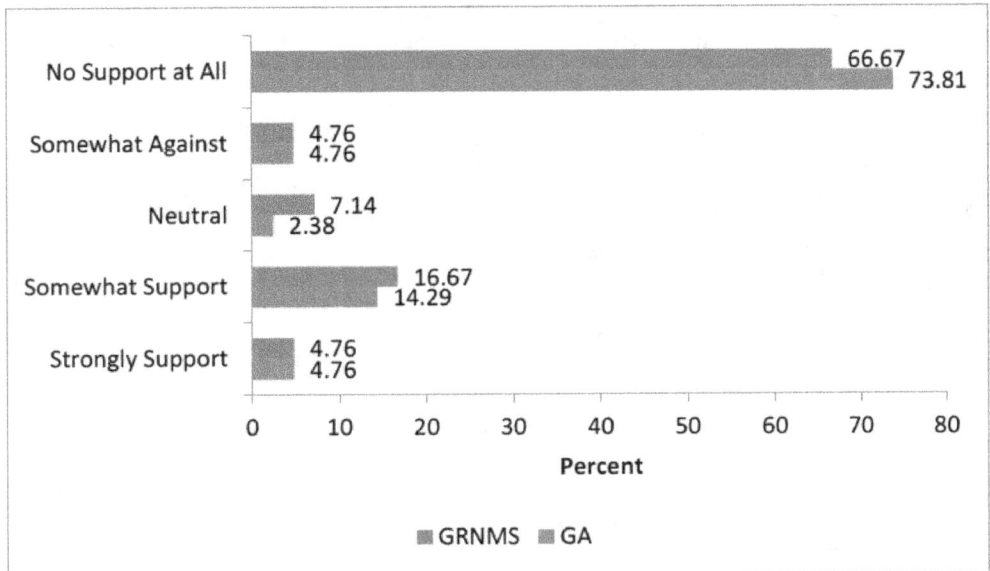

Figure 1.13 *Users' Support for Marine Reserves off the Coast of Georgia Inside versus Outside GRNMS: Version 2 Survey, 2012*

As a follow-up to the question of support for marine reserves inside GRNMS, survey respondents were asked what percent of each activity that would be displaced by marine reserves they thought would be acceptable. Nine separate uses/activities were presented that would be displaced by marine reserves in GRNMS. Users of GRNMS generally did not support marine reserves, but if they were implemented the maximum acceptable impact on user groups that would be displaced ranged from 12.8% to 40.71% (Figure 1.14).

Users of GRNMS generally don't support the uses of marine reserves off Georgia, but if they were implemented the maximum acceptable impact on user groups that would be displaced ranged from 12.38 percent to 40.71 percent.

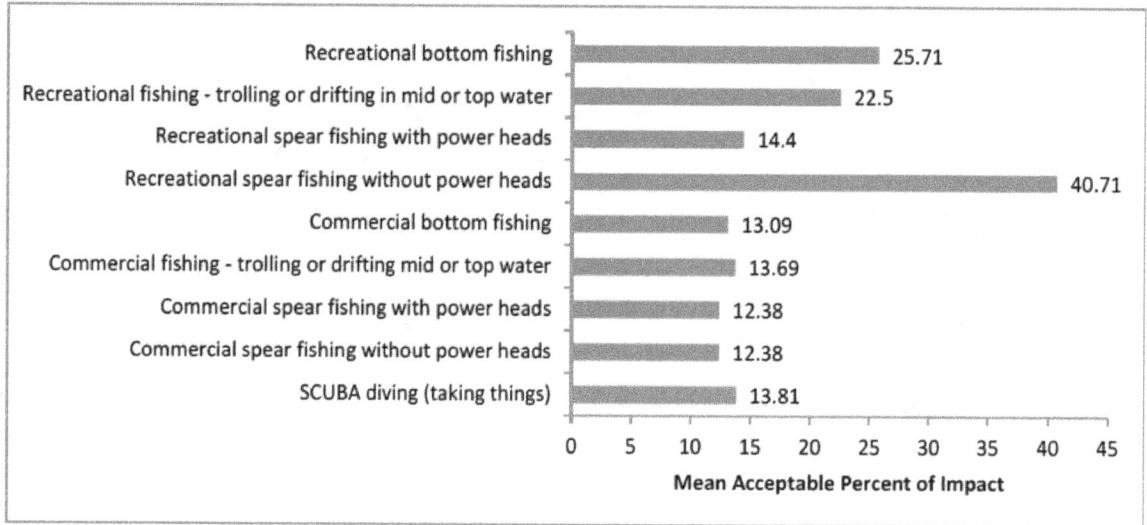

Figure 1.14 *Maximum Acceptable Impacts of Marine Reserves on Different User Groups Displaced: Users of GRNMS Version 2 Survey, 2012*

Research Only Areas

Survey respondents were asked for their level of support for research only areas in the coastal and ocean waters off Georgia outside GRNMS and inside GRNMS. The same five-point support scale that was used for marine reserves was used. An overwhelming majority of users of GRNMS showed no support at all or were somewhat against the creation of research only areas in coastal and ocean waters both inside (78.57%) and outside GRNMS (78.05%) (Figure 1.15).

An overwhelming majority of users of GRNMS do not support the use of research only areas in the coastal and ocean waters off the coast of Georgia both inside and outside GRNMS.

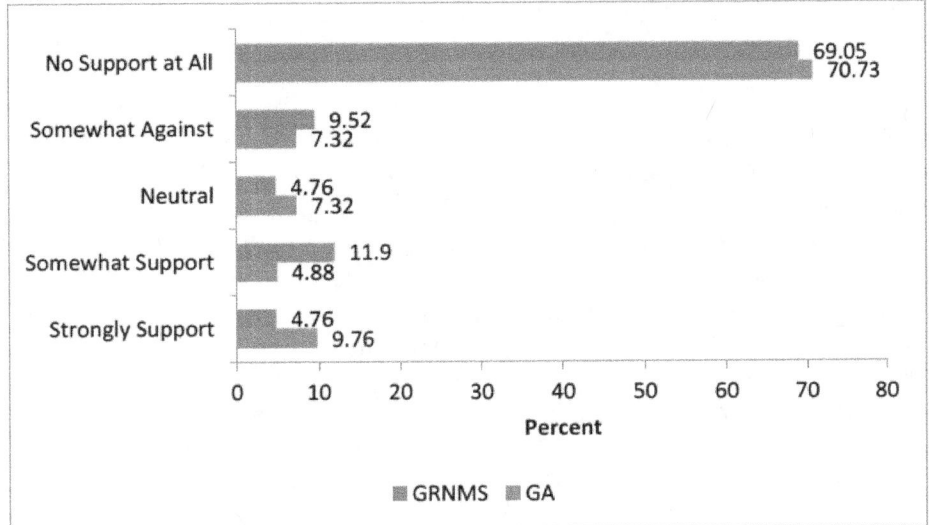

Figure 1.15 *User's Support for Research Only Areas off the Coast of Georgia inside versus Outside GRNMS: Version 2 Survey, 2012*

As a follow-up to the question of support for research only areas inside GRNMS, survey respondents were asked what percent of each activity that would be displaced by research only areas they thought would be acceptable. Eleven separate uses/activities were presented that would be displaced by research only areas in GRNMS. Users of GRNMS generally don't support the creation of research only areas in GRNMS, but if implemented the maximum acceptable impact on user groups that would be displaced would range from 16% to 24.5% of selected activities. An unexpected result was that the less consumptive an activity, the higher the accepted level of impact (Figure 1.16). One explanation for this result is that the majority of users don't engage in non-consumptive recreation so they care less about preserving access for non-consumptive users.

Users of GRNMS generally don't support the uses of research only areas off Georgia, but if they were implemented the maximum acceptable impact on user groups that would be displaced ranged from 16 percent to 24.52 percent.

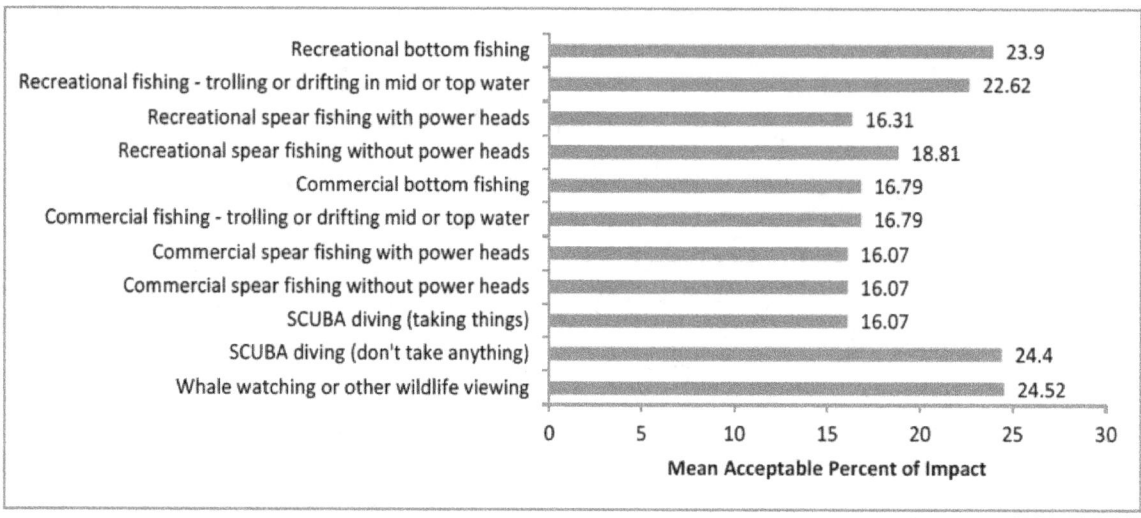

Figure 1.16 *Maximum Acceptable Impact of Research Only Areas on Different User Groups Displaced: Users of GRNMS Version 2 Survey, 2012*

Multi-species Fishery Management

Survey respondents were told that historically fishery managers or managers of marine mammals have managed on a species by species basis and recent trends are to expand this species specific approach to what is being called multi-species management. They were further told that in fisheries management, the approach involves looking at various inter-relationships between species such as predator-prey relationships (big fish eat little fish). Respondents were then asked for their level of support for the multi-species approach using the five-point Likert support scale. Only a little over one-third of users of GRNMS strongly or somewhat support the multi-species approach to fishery management. Over 38% had no support or were somewhat against it (Figure 1.17).

A plurality of users of GRNMS do not support multi-species fishery management with a little over 38 percent against it and a little more than 33 percent for it.

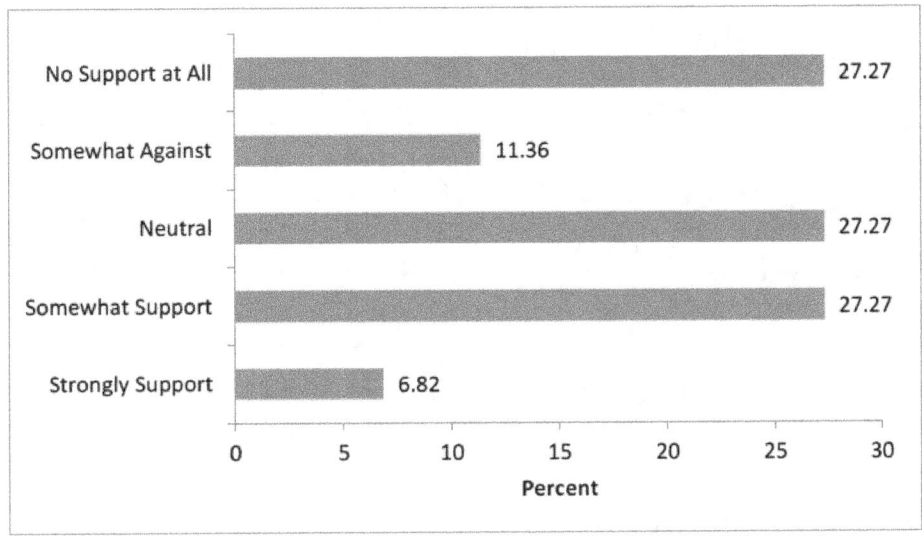

Figure 1.17 *User's Support for Multi-species Fishery Management: Version 2 Survey, 2012*

Ecosystem-based Approach to Management of Coastal and Ocean Resources

Survey respondents were told that there was a more comprehensive approach that goes beyond fishery management. They were also told that in a full ecosystem-based management approach, all human uses and values are recognized and that management attempts to achieve a balance across many different uses and values. Respondents were then asked for their level of support for the ecosystem-based management approach using the five-point Likert scale. A majority of - users of GRNMS would not support an ecosystem-based approach with more than 54% with either no support at all or somewhat against. Only 20.46% strongly or somewhat supported this approach (Figure 1.18).

A majority of users of GRNMS do not support ecosystem-based management. Only a little more than 20 percent support this management approach.

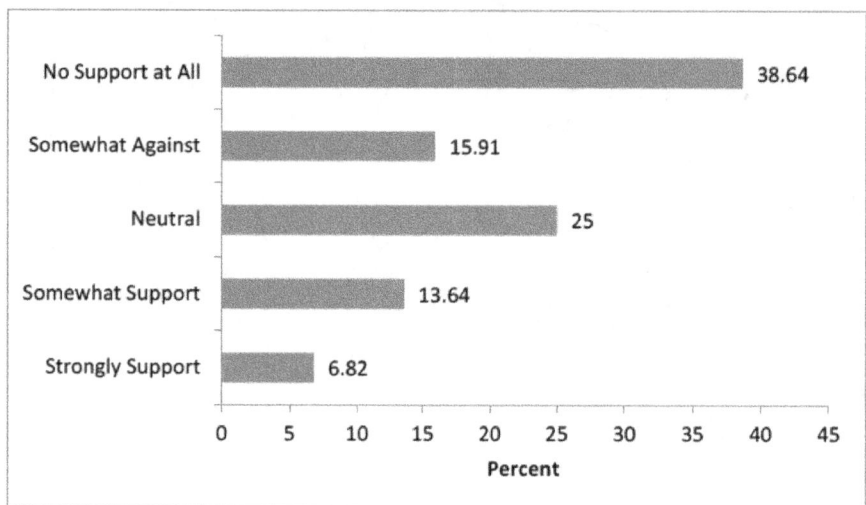

Figure 1.18 *User's Support for Ecosystem-based Management: Version 2 Survey, 2012*

CHAPTER 2: USERS OF GRNMS VERSIONS 1 AND 2 POOLED

This chapter pools the responses received from the version 1 survey conducted in 2011 and version 2 conducted in 2012 for information asked in both versions of the surveys. This includes user profiles for respondents, which include the demographic profiles of users, membership in organizations, boat ownership, activity participation and use, and the factors that determined the choice of using GRNMS. The profiles are followed by user's sources of information used, level of trust for sources of information used, and the perceptions of the status of resource conditions in GRNMS.

The pooled sample includes a total of 121 respondents. Of the 121 responses, 33 responded to both versions 1 and 2. Six of the 21 new users added to our list of users responded to version 2 and five users that did not respond to version 1 responded to version 2.

For the 33 respondents that responded to versions 1 and 2, we used their responses to version 2 for the pooled data results. We first did tests for statistical differences between the responses in the two versions for these 33 respondents. There were some differences but very few statistically significant differences. There were no statistically significant differences in demographics, activity participation and use, membership in organizations, boat ownership, factors that determined the choice of using GRNMS or status of resource conditions in GRNMS. There were a couple of statistically significant differences for sources of information used and the level of trust for a couple of information sources used. See Leeworthy (2013) for results of the statistical tests.

User Profiles

Demographics

The survey questionnaire included demographic information on the survey respondent's sex, age, race/ethnicity, educational attainment, employment status, household income, household type, and household size. Users were all white non-Hispanic males with ages ranging from 24 to 76 years (mean 53.72 and median 54) (Table 2.1).

Table 2.1. Sex, Race/Ethnicity, and Age of GRNMS Users: Pooled 2011-2012 Surveys

Sex	100% male		
Race/Ethnicity	100% Non Hispanic White		
Age			
Mean	53.72		
Median	54		
Minimum	24		
Maximum	76		

Users had generally high levels of educational attainment with almost 71 percent with "Some College" or above (Figure 2.1). None of the users were unemployed during the 2011/2012 survey period with about 70% employed full-time and more than 19% retired (Figure 2.2). Users also had relatively high household incomes with half of household incomes over $100,000 (Figure 2.3). Almost 71% of users lived in households without children (Figure 2.4). About 62% lived in households with two people or less (Figure 2.5) with an average household size of 2.56 (Table 2.2).

> Users of GRNMS had generally high levels of educational attainment with almost 71 percent with some college or above.

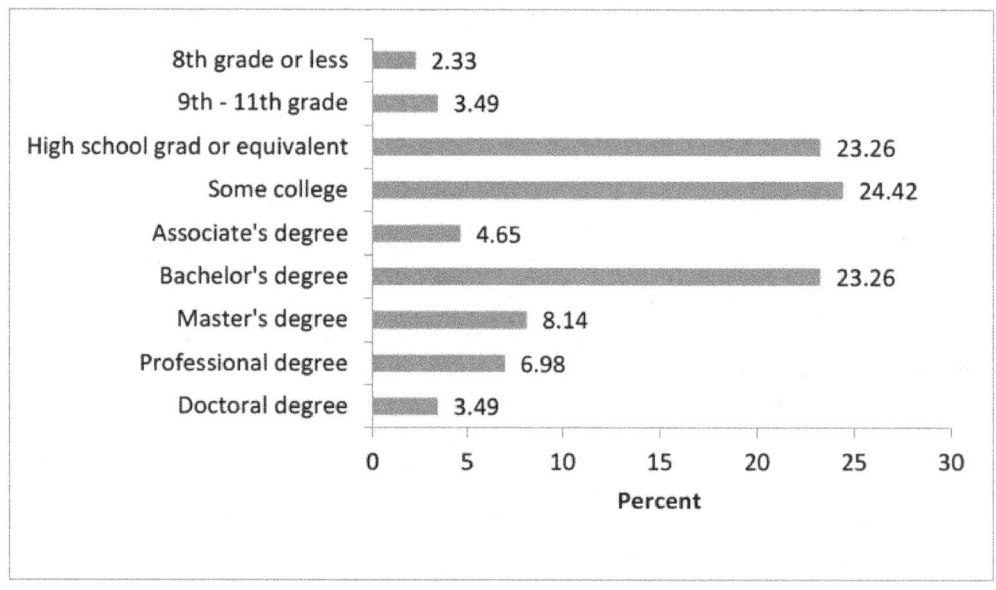

Figure 2.1 *Educational Attainment of Users: Pooled 2011-2012 Surveys.*

About 70 percent of GRNMS users were employed full-time with zero unemployed and more than 19 percent retired.

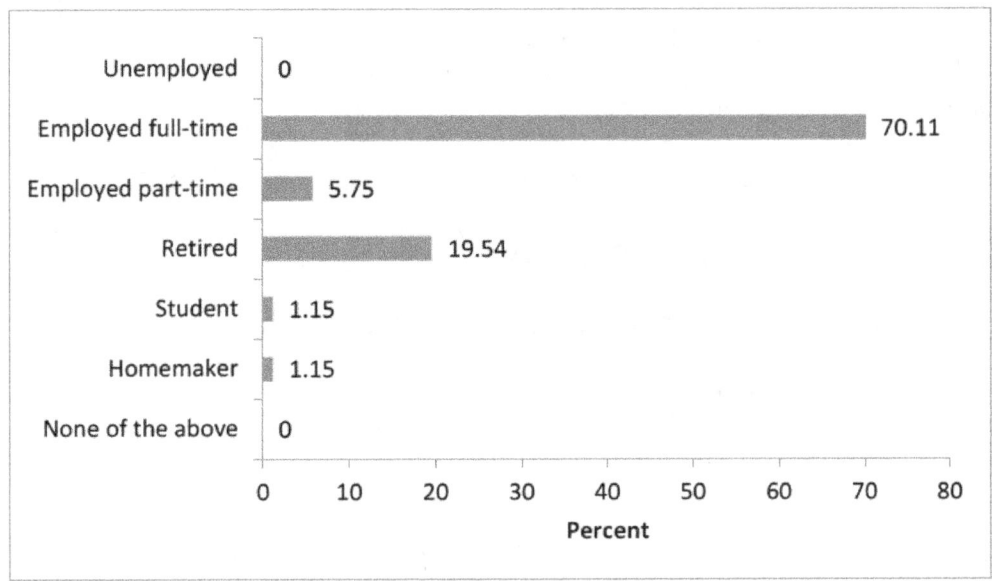

Figure 2.2 *Employment Status of Users: Pooled 2011-2012 Surveys*

Users of GRNMS had relatively high household incomes with half having incomes over $100,000.

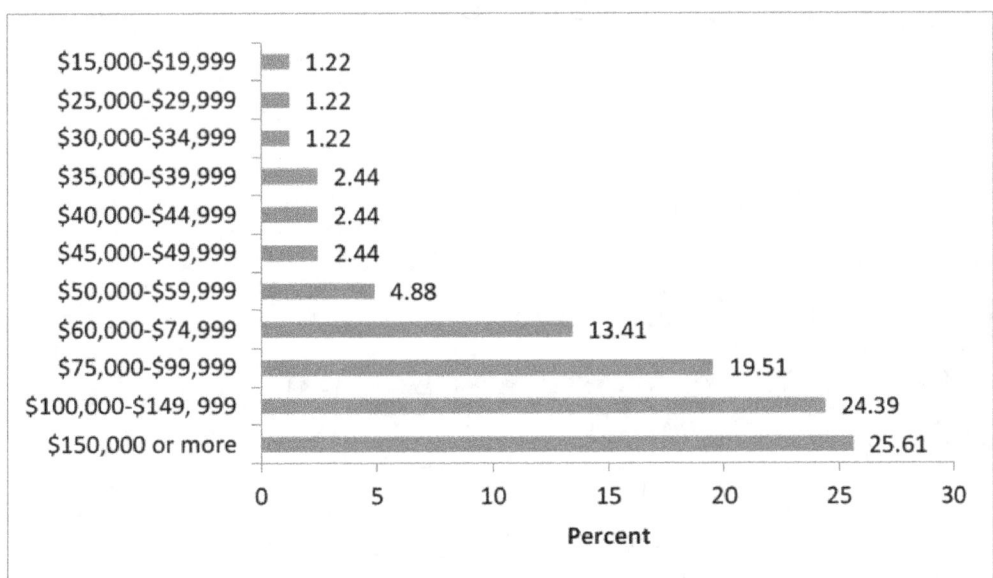

Figure 2.3 *Household Income before Taxes of Users: Pooled 2011-2012 Surveys*

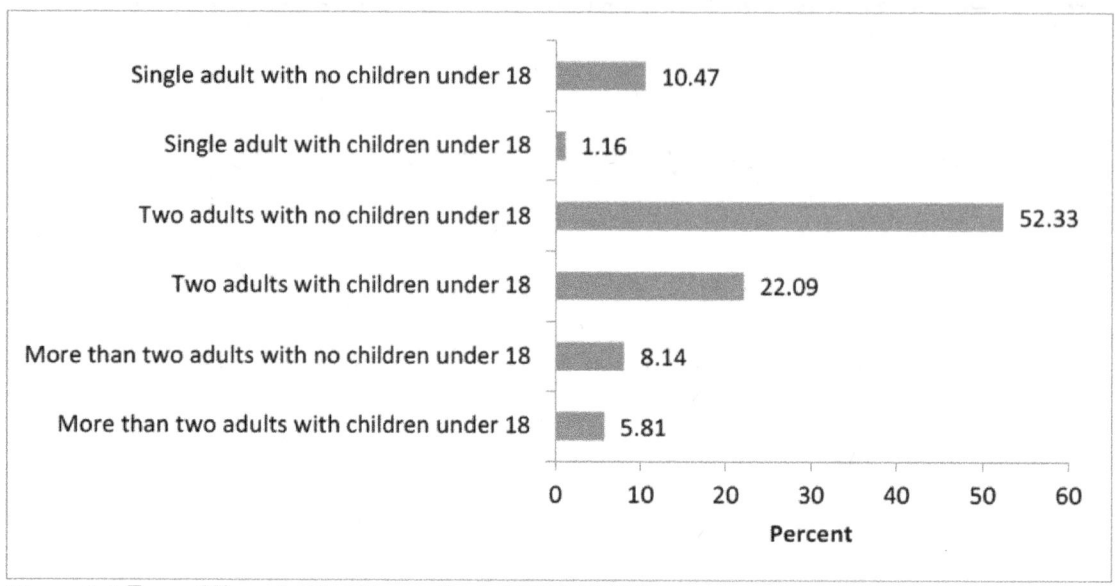

Figure 2.4 *Type of Household of Users: Pooled 2011-2012 Surveys*

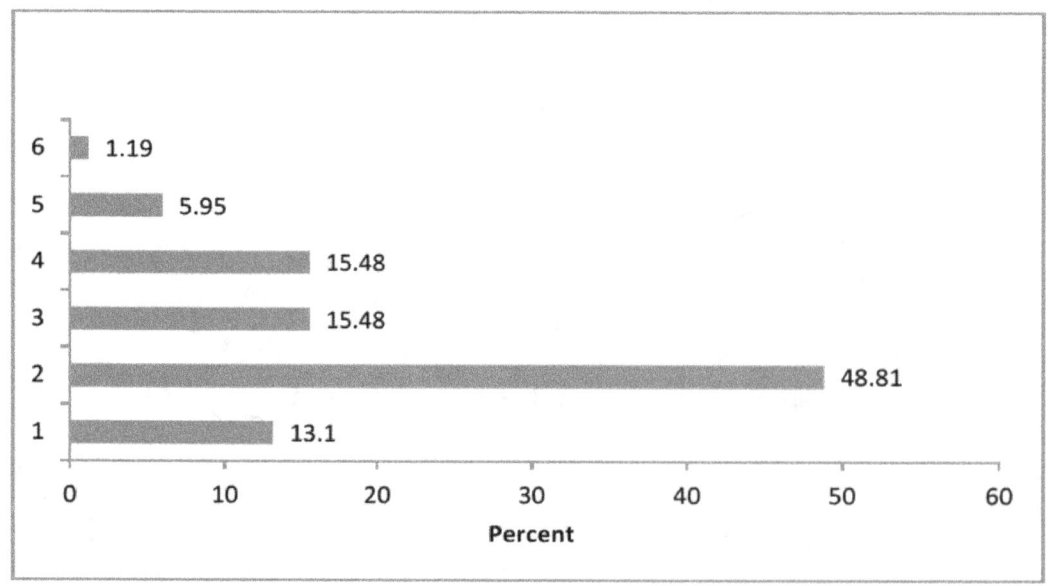

Figure 2.5 *Household Size of Users: Pooled 2011-2012 Surveys*

Table 2.2. Household Size: Users of GRNMS Pooled 2011-2012 Surveys

	Mean	Median	Minimum	Maximum
Total Household Size	2.56	2	1	6
Number age 18 or older	2.03	2	1	4
Number under age 18	0.51	0	0	5

Organizational Membership and Boat Ownership

More than 44% of all users were members of fishing groups, clubs or organizations, while almost 11% were members of chambers of commerce. Also, 8% were members of environmental groups (Figure 2.6).

More than 44 percent of users of GRNMS were members of fishing groups, clubs or organizations, while 11 percent were members of chambers of commerce.

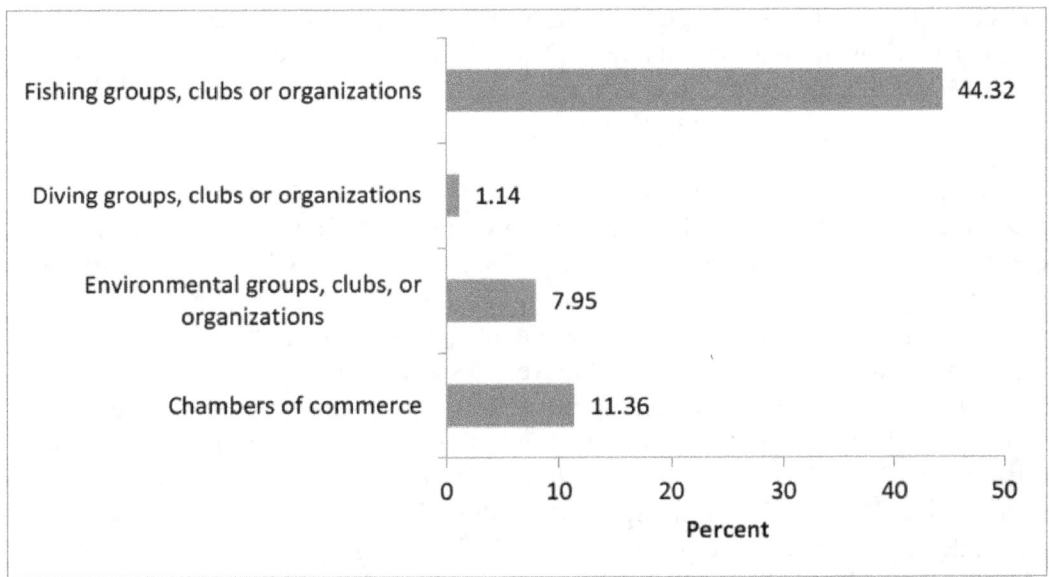

Figure 2.6 *User's Memberships in Groups, Clubs and Organizations: Pooled 2011-2012 Surveys*

More than 97% of users owned a boat ranging from 16 to 47 feet in length (mean 24.47 feet). On average, about three people were aboard the boats when in GRNMS (Table 2.3).

Table 2.3. Boat Ownership, Length of Boat, and Number of People Aboard: Users
        of GRNMS Pooled 2011-2012 Surveys

Do you own a boat? (percent yes)	97.67
Length of Boat Owned (feet)	
Mean	24.47
Median	23.5
Minimum	16
Maximun	47
Number of People Aboard	
Mean	3.1
Median	3
Minimum	1
Maximum	5

Activity Participation and Use

The survey gathered information on recreation activities that users participated in at GRNMS
and in coastal and ocean areas of Georgia outside GRNMS. Activities were classified as those
that take place in GRNMS and those that do not take place in GRNMS, but do take place in
coastal and ocean areas of Georgia outside GRNMS.

Participation in activities that take place in GRNMS - The survey asked about participation in
"recreational bottom fishing", "recreational fishing–trolling or drifting in mid or top water",
"recreational spear fishing with power heads", "recreational spear fishing without power heads",
"SCUBA diving (don't take anything)", "SCUBA diving (taking things)", "Whale watching or
other wildlife viewing activities" and "Sailing". These activities were then classified into
"consumptive" and "nonconsumptive" activities. Figure 2.7 summarizes the results. Users of
GRNMS had higher participation rates in consumptive activities than in nonconsumptive
activities in the coastal and ocean waters off Georgia, including GRNMS. About 93%
participated in fishing in GRNMS and 95% participated in fishing in the coastal and ocean
waters of Georgia outside GRNMS. Even though spear fishing is prohibited in GRNMS, about
6% of survey respondents said they participated in spear fishing in GRNMS, while more than
13% said they did it in coastal and ocean areas of Georgia outside GRNMS. About 8%
participated in SCUBA diving in GRNMS, while about 17% participated in SCUBA diving in
the coastal and ocean waters of Georgia outside GRNMS.

For activities that are known to occur in GRNMS, users of GRNMS had higher participation rates in consumptive activities than nonconsumptive activities in the coastal and ocean waters off Georgia, with 93 and 95 percent participating in fishing in either GRNMS or coastal and ocean waters outside GRNMS off the Georgia coast.

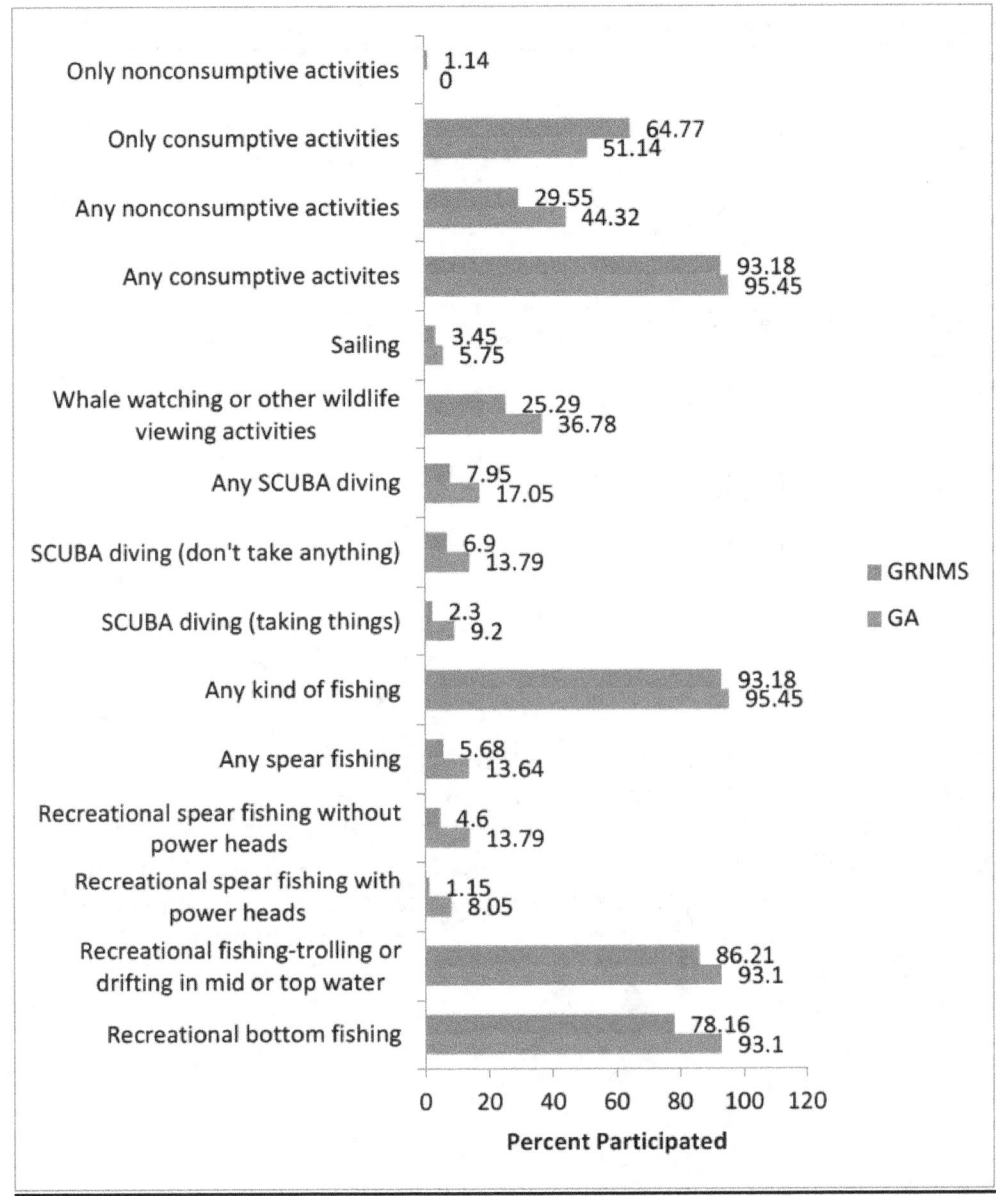

Figure 2.7 *User's Activity Participation in GA and GRNMS: Pooled 2011-2012 Surveys*

Participation in activities that don't take place in GRNMS - The survey asked about participation in "Beach activities", "Surfing", "Windsurfing or kite boarding", "Personal watercraft use (jet skis, wave runners, etc.)", and "Shorebird watching". Users of GRNMS had the highest participation in "Beach activities" with 80.46% and "Shorebird watching" with 31.18%. More than 18% participated in "Personal watercraft use", while more than 11% participated in surfing and a little more than 8% in "windsurfing or kite boarding" (Figure 2.8).

> For selected activities that don't occur in GRNMS, users of GRNMS had the highest participation in beach and shorebird watching activities in the coastal and ocean waters off Georgia outside GRNMS.

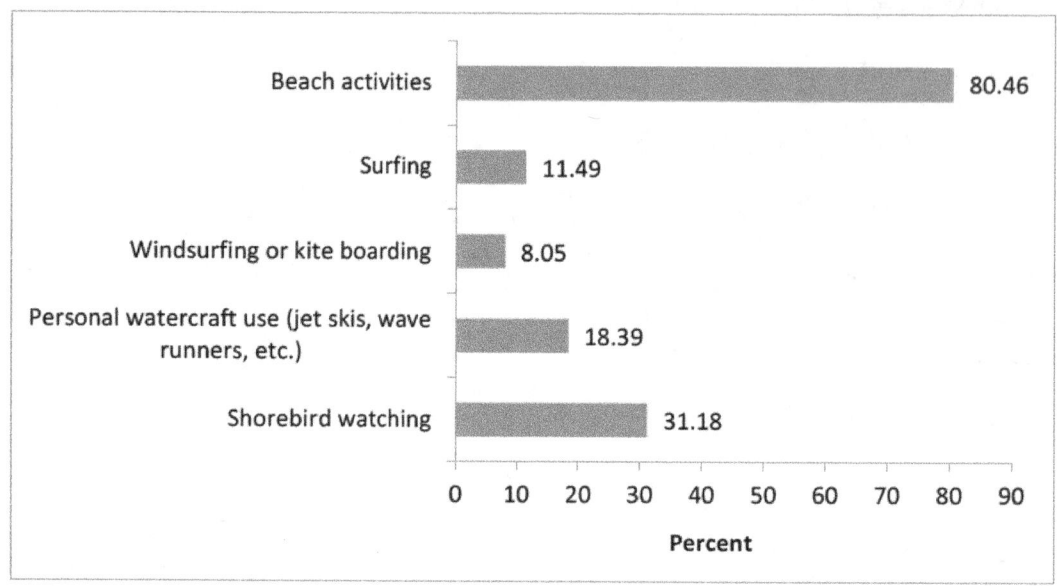

Figure 2.8 *User's Activity Participation in GA for Selected Activities: Pooled 2011-2012 Surveys*

Person-days of use by activity - Intensity of use was measured as annual person-days of use where a person-day is equal to one person doing an activity for a whole day or any part of a day. Survey respondents were asked about their use for the activities that take place in GRNMS and how many person-days were in GRNMS versus how many person-days were in coastal and ocean waters of Georgia outside GRNMS. Results were summarized as the mean number of person-days for "all users", which includes those that did zero days of an activity, and "participants only", which includes only those that did at least one day of an activity (Table 2.4).

Table 2.4. Person-days of Activity Participation in GA and GRNMS: Users of GRNMS Pooled 2011-2012

| Activity | All Users[1] | | Participants Only | |
	GA (mean)	GRNMS (mean)	GA (mean)	GRNMS (mean)
Recreational bottom fishing	25.52	9.51	27.46	12.38
Recreational fishing - trolling or drfting in mid or top water	17.93	8.29	19.34	9.78
Recreational spear fishing with power heads	0.27	0.00	5.75	0.00
Recreational spear fishing without power heads	0.38	0.06	4.00	2.50
SCUBA diving (taking things)	0.09	0.07	3.50	6.00
SCUBA diving (don't take things)	0.36	0.13	4.29	2.75
Whale watching or other wildlife viewing activities	3.57	1.45	11.44	7.73

1. All Users includes people who did not do the activity, so they have zero days of use.
* sample size too small

Outside GRNMS, users had the highest mean person-days of activity in "recreational bottom fishing" at 25.52 person-days in 2011/2012, while "recreational fishing-trolling or drifting in mid or top water" was second with 17.93 person-days. This difference was statistically significant (Table 2.4).

Inside GRNMS, users had the highest mean person-days of activity in "recreational bottom fishing" with 9.51 person-days for 2011/2012, while "recreational fishing – trolling or drifting in mid or top water" was close behind with 8.29 person-days. The difference, however, is not statistically significant (Table 2.4).

Participation in fishing tournaments - Survey respondents, who fished were asked if they participated in fishing tournaments. About 37% participated in fishing tournaments (Figure 2.9).

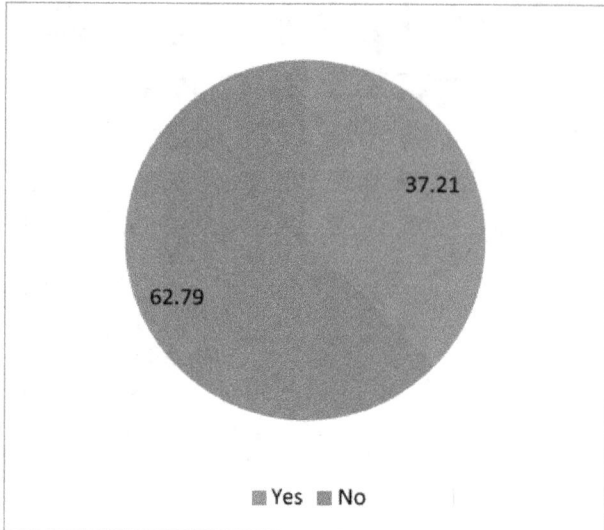

Figure 2.9 User's Participation in Fishing Tournaments: Pooled 2011-2012 Surveys

Factors Influencing the Choice of Going to GRNMS for Activities

Survey respondents were asked for the factors that influenced their choices when deciding to go to GRNMS for their activities. For each factor they were asked to respond either "Yes", "Somewhat", or "Not at All". "Sea conditions" had the highest proportions of users who said "Yes" with 81.93%. This was followed by "Fish species preference" (75.90%), "Weather" (73.49%), "Seasonal patterns" (66.67%) and "Distance to GRNMS" (60.00%). Even though about 93% fish in GRNMS, only 50.00% said "Yes" to "better fishing" (Table 2.5).

Table 2.5. Factors Influencing Choice of Going to GRNMS for Activities: Pooled 2011-12 Surveys

Factor	Yes (%)	Somewhat (%)	Not at All (%)	
Weather	73.49	22.89	3.61	
Fish species preference	75.90	16.87	7.23	
Time of Day	48.68	26.32	25.00	
Seasonal patterns	66.67	28.21	5.13	
Word of mouth/radio talk	38.67	34.67	26.67	
Boat Captain's choice	38.03	15.49	46.48	
Sea conditions	81.93	13.25	4.82	
Distance to GRNMS	60.00	26.25	13.75	
Better fishing	50.00	43.75	6.25	
Better diving for things to see	12.50	10.71	76.79	

Knowledge

The survey addressed four topics on knowledge; 1) sources of information used, 2) level of trust of information sources used, 3) how users prefer to receive information about GRNMS and 4) familiarity with GRNMS regulations. The "Don't Know" responses to the attitudes and perceptions questions also provide indirect information about user's knowledge.

Sources of Information Used

The survey asked about 22 known possible sources of information and provided for other sources responses. The most used sources of information included the "Georgia Department of Natural Resources" (67.44%), "Internet" (63.95%), "Word of mouth" (59.30%), "GRNMS web site" (53.49%), "Fishing magazines/newsletters" (51.16%), "NOAA's National Marine Fisheries Service" (48.84%), "Newspapers" (45.35%), "Marinas" (42.85%), and the "Southern Kingfish Association" (41.86%). Only 11.90% had used "Social media (Twitter, You Tube, Facebook, etc.). The full results are summarized in Table 2.6.

Table 2.6. Sources of Information Used about GRNMS: Users of GRNMS Pooled 2011-2012
Surveys

Source	Used (% Yes)
Grays Reef National Marine Sanctuary Sanctuary Advisory Council	15.12
Grays Reef National Marine Sanctuary Staff	16.28
Grays Reef National Marine Sanctuary Web site	53.49
NOAA's National Marine Fisheries Service	48.84
Atlantic States Marine fisheries Commission	11.63
South Atlantic Fishery Management Council	11.63
Georgia Department of Natural Resources	67.44
Georgia Sea Grant	6.98
Coastal Conservation Association of Georgia (CCAGA)	26.74
Recreational Fishing Alliance (RFA)	29.07
American Sportfishing Association (ASA)	22.09
National Coalition for Marine Conservation (NCMC)	4.65
International Game and Fish Association (IGFA)	24.42
Southern Kingfish Association (SKA)	41.86
Fishing Magazines/Newsletters	51.16
SCUBA diving magazines/Newsletters	17.44
Newspapers	45.35
Radio	26.74
Television	38.37
Internet	63.95
Social Media (Twitter, You tube, Facebook, etc.)	11.90
Word of mouth	59.30
Marinas	42.85
Fishing Captains	7.14
Other Anglers	21.43
Other Divers	7.14

Level of Trust of Information Sources Used

For sources of information used, respondents were asked for their level of trust of the information scored on a five-point Likert scale where 1=No Trust at All and 5=Completely Trust. For the sources that were used the most, the Southern Kingfish Association had the highest level of trust with 88.23% trusting it very much or completely trusted. The "Georgia Department of Natural Resources" followed with 76.67% trusting it very much or completely trusting, and "GRNMS web site" with 62.79% trusting it very much or completely trusting. Although the "Internet" and "Word of mouth" were highly used sources of information, only 32.7% trusted very much or completely trusted the "Internet", while only 44% trusted very much or completely trusted "Word of mouth" (Table 2.7).

Table 2.7. Level of Trust of Information Sources Used: Users of GRNMS Pooled 2011-2012 Surveys

Source	No Trust\ At All	Very Little Trust	Neutral	Trust Very Much	Completely Trust
Grays Reef National Marine Sanctuary Advisory Council	25.00	8.33	8.33	58.33	0.00
Grays Reef National Marine Sanctuary Staff	23.08	7.69	15.38	46.15	7.69
Grays Reef National Marine Sanctuary Web site	2.33	16.28	18.60	48.84	13.95
NOAA's National Marine Fisheries Service	10.26	7.69	17.95	43.59	20.51
Atlantic States Marine Fisheries Commission	20.00	60.00	0.00	20.00	0.00
South Atlantic Fishery Management Council	20.00	40.00	0.00	40.00	0.00
Georgia Department of Natural Resources	3.92	9.80	19.61	51.18	25.49
Georgia Sea Grant	16.67	0.00	50.00	33.33	0.00
Coastal Conservation Association of Georgia (CCAGA)	0.00	0.00	4.35	65.22	30.43
Recreational Fishing Alliance (RFA)	0.00	0.00	8.33	70.83	20.83
American Sportfishing Association (ASA)	0.00	0.00	11.76	64.71	23.53
National Coalition for Marine Conservation (NCMC)	0.00	0.00	50.00	50.00	0.00
International Game and Fish Association (IGFA)	0.00	0.00	15.00	65.00	20.00
Southern Kingfish Association (SKA)	0.00	2.94	8.82	58.82	29.41
Fishing Magazines/Newsletters	0.00	5.00	35.00	57.50	2.50
SCUBA diving magazines/Newsletters	0.00	0.00	25.00	75.00	0.00
Newspapers	0.00	5.71	54.29	31.43	8.57
Radio	0.00	0.00	60.00	30.00	10.00
Television	0.00	6.45	48.39	41.94	3.23
Internet	0.00	7.69	59.62	28.85	3.85
Social Media (Twitter, You tube, Facebook, etc.)	0.00	11.11	77.78	11.11	0.00
Word of mouth	0.00	8.89	46.67	35.55	8.89

How Users Would Like to Receive Information about GRNMS

Backing up the sources of information used and the level of trust of the sources used, the "GRNMS web site" was chosen as the most preferred way users would like to receive information about GRNMS at 55.17%. A "Newsletter delivered by the U.S. Postal Service" was preferred by 48.28% closely followed by "E-mail list serve" with 47.67%. A "Telephone call from staff" was the least preferred at 9.3% (Figure 2.10).

Most users of GRNMS would prefer to receive information about GRNMS via either the GRNMS web site, newsletter delivered to their home via the U.S. Postal Service, or E-mail list serve.

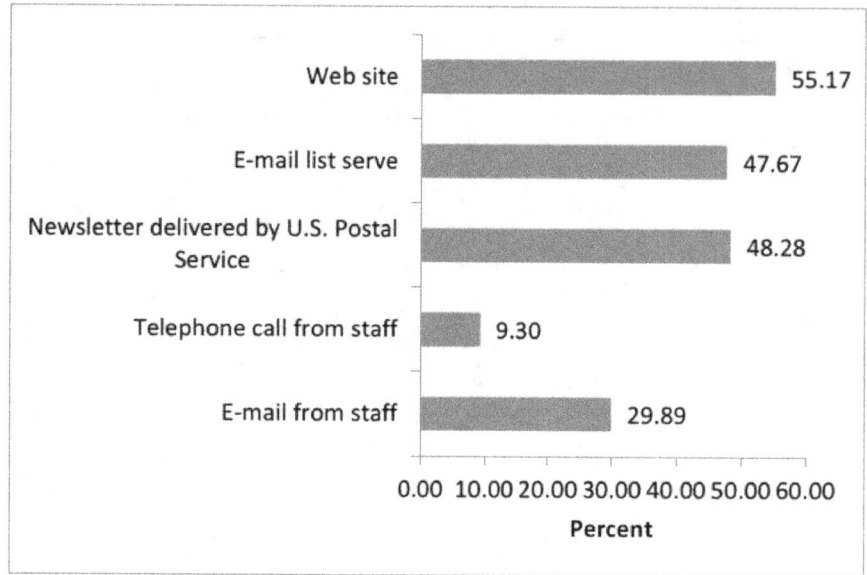

Figure 2.10 *How Users would like to receive information about GRNMS: Pooled 2011-2012 Surveys*

Familiarity with GRNMS Regulations

Survey respondents were also asked for a self-evaluation of their familiarity with the regulations of GRNMS. More than 72% of users said they were "somewhat familiar" with the regulations and more than 20% said they were "very familiar" with the regulations. Only 6.9% said they were not at all familiar with the regulations (Figure 2.11).

Over 93 percent of users of GRNMS were familiar with GRNMS rules and regulations.

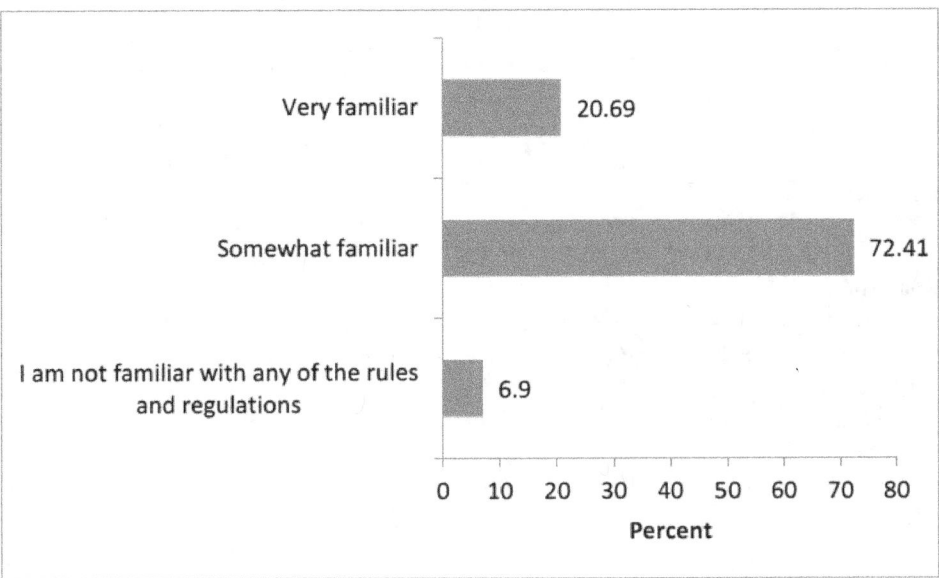

Figure 2.11 *User's Familiarity with GRNMS Rules and Regulations: Pooled 2011-2012 Surveys*

Perceptions

The survey asked users for their perceptions of conditions of 11 resources in GRNMS. Ratings of conditions were asked using a five-point Likert scale with 1=getting a lot better, 2=getting somewhat better, 3=same, 4=getting somewhat worse, and 5=getting a lot worse. A "Don't Know" response was also allowed. A high proportion of users responded that they "Don't Know" for all 11 resources. For all resources, except "Invasive species" a higher proportion of users thought conditions were getting somewhat to a lot better than those who thought conditions were getting somewhat to a lot worse (Table 2.8).

Table 2.8. Perceptions of Conditions of Resources in GRNMS: Users of GRNMS Pooled 2011-2012 Surveys

Resource	Getting a Lot Better	Getting Somewhat Better	Same	Getting Somewhat Worse	Getting a Lot Worse	Don't Know
Live bottom habitat	11.49	22.99	29.89	4.60	1.15	29.89
Other bottom habitat	9.20	21.84	34.48	5.75	0.00	28.74
Fish populations (bottom fish)	13.95	26.74	27.91	9.30	0.00	22.09
Fish populations (pelagic)	12.64	18.39	35.63	12.64	3.45	17.24
Fish populations (diversity or number of species)	11.49	17.24	43.68	6.90	0.00	20.69
Other Sea life (abundance)	10.34	22.99	32.18	3.45	1.15	29.89
Other Sea life (diversity or number of species)	8.14	23.26	37.21	2.33	0.00	29.07
Water quality	9.20	16.09	43.68	6.90	0.00	24.14
Invasive species (such as lionfish)	1.15	2.30	20.69	18.39	14.94	42.53
Marine debris (plastics, other trash)	6.90	17.24	28.74	18.39	3.45	25.29
Sea based pollution (discharges from boats)	8.05	14.94	40.23	9.20	4.60	22.99

CHAPTER 3: USER AND NON-USER COMPARISONS VERSION 2

In this chapter, users and non-users of GRNMS who responded to version 2 of the surveys are compared and statistically significant differences are highlighted. Version 2 of the users and the non-user surveys included profiles, which included demographics and activity participation and use. Version 2 also included concern for health of coastal and ocean resources off the Georgia coast inside and outside GRNMS and support for various management strategies inside and outside GRNMS.

User Profiles

Demographics

Users were significantly different from non-users for every demographic factor except educational attainment and average household size. Users were all male, while for non-users the proportion of males was closer to the general population of Georgia (Figure 3.1). Users were all white, while the distribution by race for non-users was closer to the general population of Georgia (Figure 3.2). Users were, on average, significantly older than non-users, and users were more concentrated in the age range of 50 to 64 than non-users (Table 3.1 and Figure 3.3). Although there appear to be some differences in educational attainment between users and non-users, the differences are not statistically significant (Figure 3.4). Users had significantly higher household incomes than non-users. No user had a household income less than $25,000, while 28.86% of non-users did. And 51.22% of users had household incomes $100,000 or above, while only 15.65% of non-users did (Figure 3.5). None of the users were unemployed, while 35.19% of non-users were. Further, 68% of users were employed full-time, while only about 42% of non-users were employed full-time (Figure 3.6). Although non-users had higher average household size than users, the difference was not statistically significant (Table 3.2). Users were significantly more concentrated in households with two people and had a significantly lower proportion in single-person households than non-users (Figures 3.7 and 3.8).

Users of GRNMS were all males, while the distribution by sex for non-users was closer to the general population of GA.

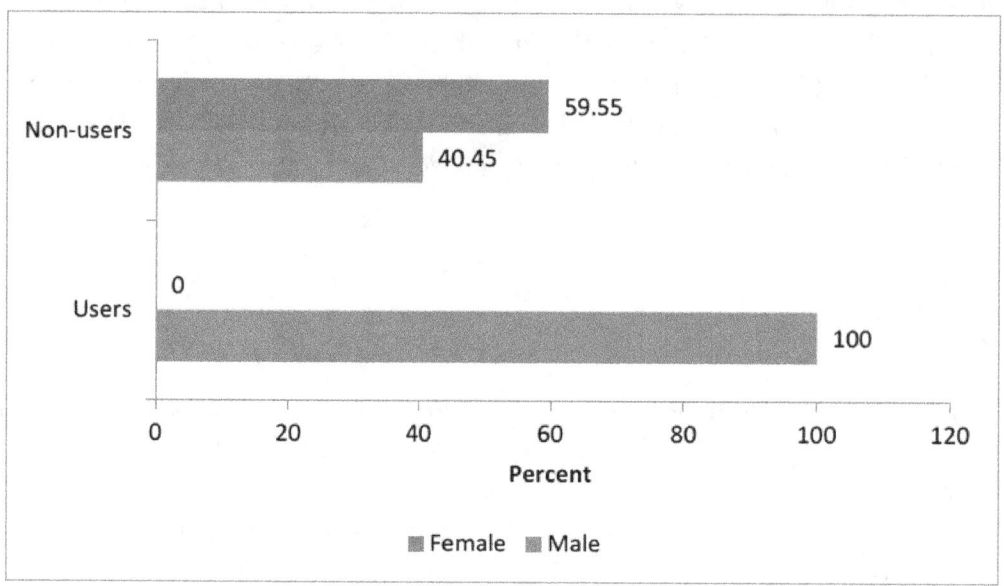

Figure 3.1 *Sex of Users versus Non-users of GRNMS: Version 2 Surveys*

Users of GRNMS were all white, while the distribution by race for non-users was closer to the general population of GA.

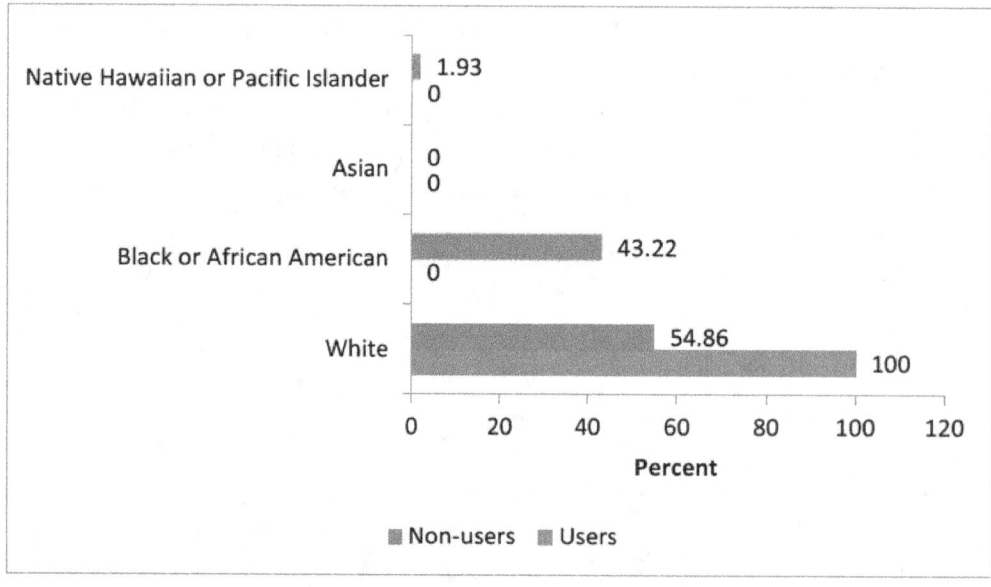

Figure 3.2 *Race of Users versus Non-users of GRNMS: Version 2 Surveys*

Table 3.1. Age of Users versus Non-users of GRNMS: Version 2 Surveys

	Mean	Median	Minimum	Maximum	Statistically Significant Difference[1]
Users	56.59	57	34	76	Yes
Non-users	42.67	39	23	96	

1. Statistical test is a t-test at .05 level of significance.

Users of GRNMS were more concentrated in the age range of 50 to 64 than non-users

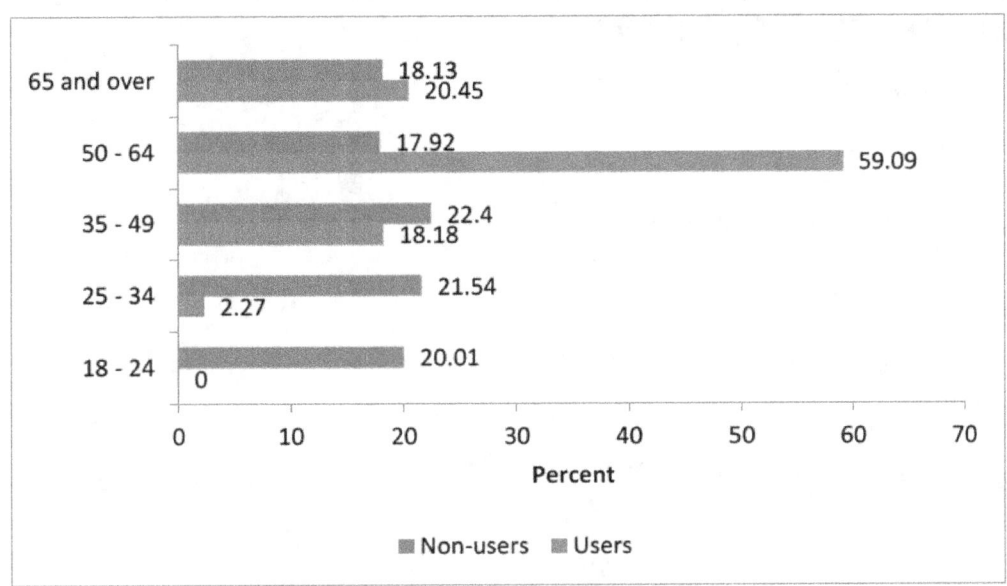

Figure 3.3 *Age of Users versus Non-users of GRNMS: Version 2 Surveys*

Although there appear to be some differences in educational attainment between users and non-users, the differences are not statistically significant.

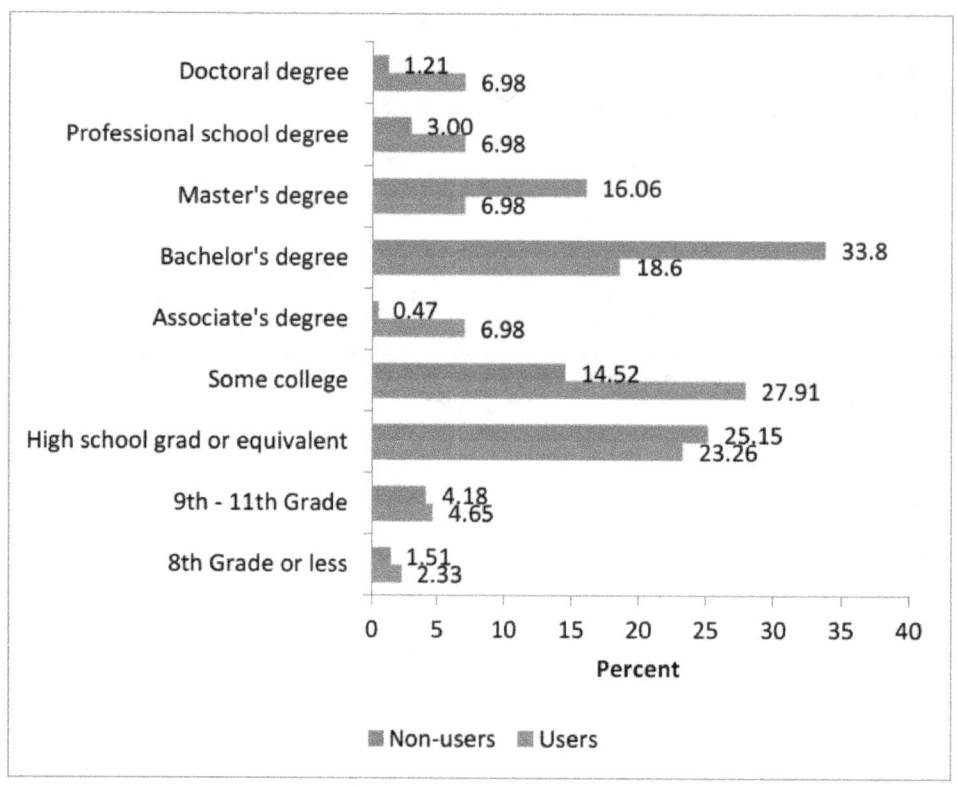

Doctoral degree — 1.21 / 6.98
Professional school degree — 3.00 / 6.98
Master's degree — 16.06 / 6.98
Bachelor's degree — 33.8 / 18.6
Associate's degree — 0.47 / 6.98
Some college — 14.52 / 27.91
High school grad or equivalent — 25.15 / 23.26
9th - 11th Grade — 4.18 / 4.65
8th Grade or less — 1.51 / 2.33

Percent

Non-users   Users

Figure 3.4 *Educational Attainment of Users versus Non-users: Version 2 Surveys*

Users had significantly higher household incomes than non-users.

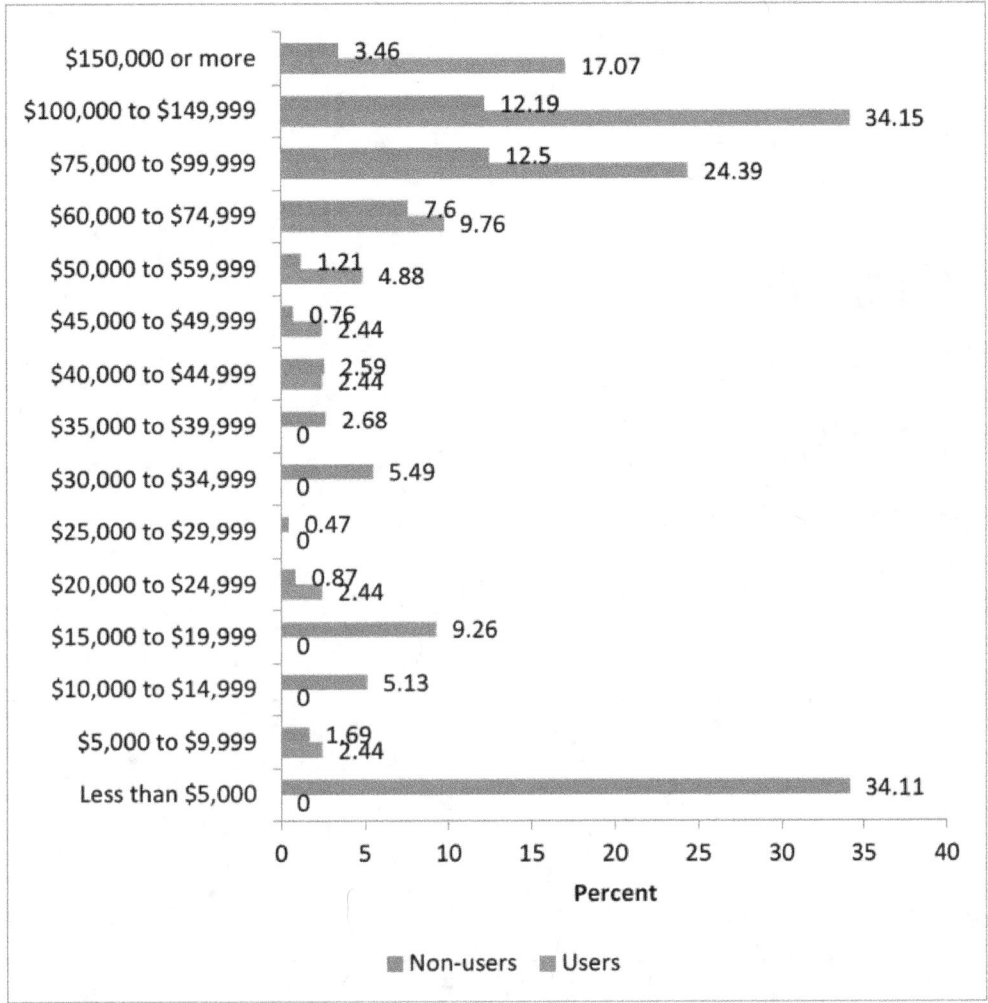

Figure 3.5 *Household Income before Taxes of Users versus Non-users: Version 2 Surveys*

Users had significantly higher rates of full-time employment and significantly lower rates of unemployment than non-users.

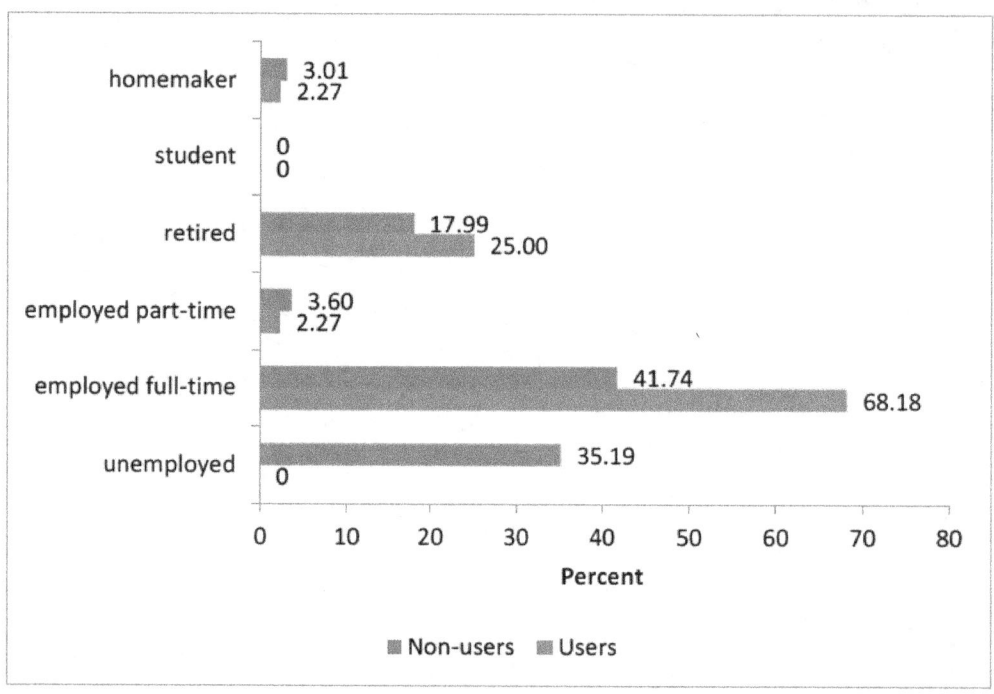

Figure 3.6 *Employment Status of Users versus Non-users: Version 2 Surveys*

Table 2.2. Household Size: Users of GRNMS Pooled 2011-2012 Surveys				
	Mean	Median	Minimum	Maximum
Total Household Size	2.56	2	1	6
Number age 18 or older	2.03	2	1	4
Number under age 18	0.51	0	0	5

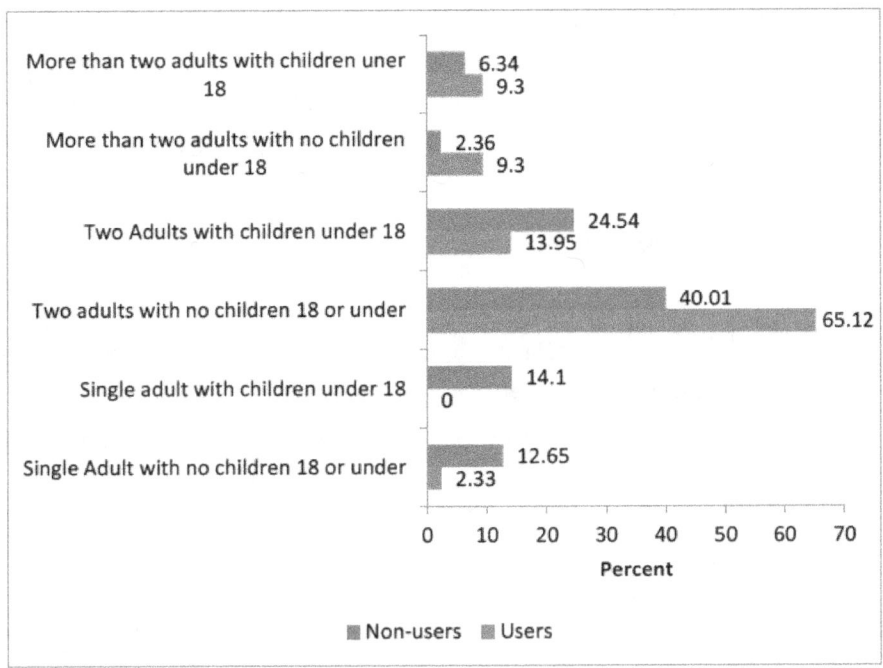

Figure 3.7 *Type of Household of Users versus Non-users: Version 2 Surveys*

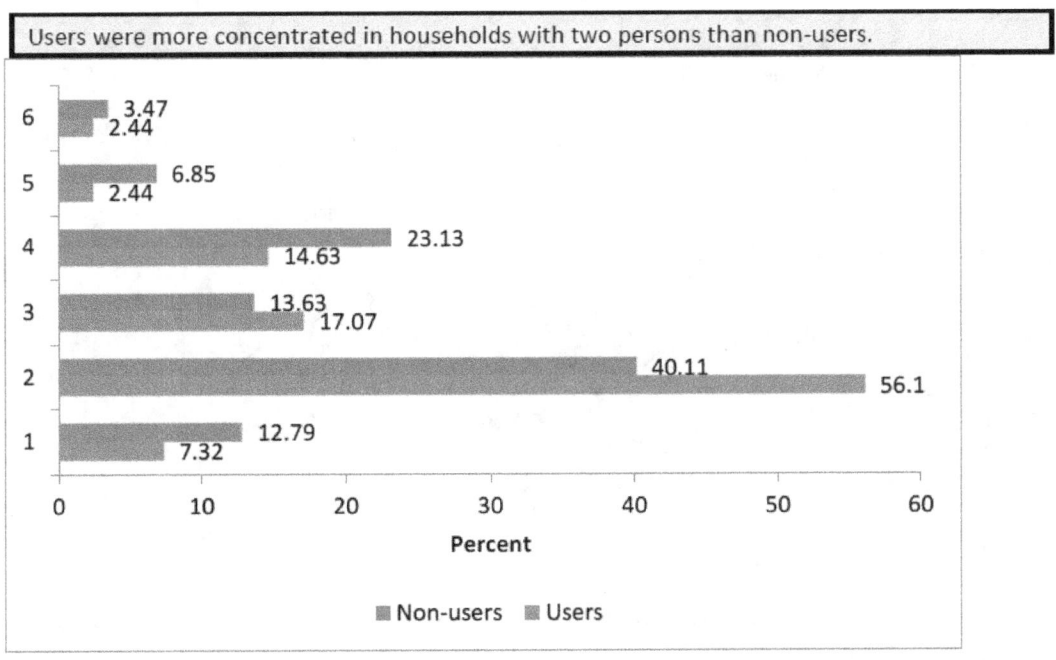

Figure 3.8 *Household Size of Users versus Non-users: Version 2 Surveys*

Organizational Membership and Boat Ownership

Users had significantly higher rates of organizational membership than non-users in fishing organizations and chambers of commerce (Figure 3.9). Users had significantly higher rates of boat ownership than non-users, 97.67% for users and 14.36% for non-users (Figure 3.10), and had, on average, bigger boats, 24.07 feet in length for users and 17.34 feet for non-users (Table 3.3).

Table 3.3. Boat Length, Users versus Non-users of GRNMS (feet): Version 2 Surveys

	Mean	Median	Minimum	Maximum	Statistically Significant Difference[1]
Users	24.07	23.00	16	35	Yes
Non-users	17.34	15.00	12	24	

1. Statistical test is a t-test at .05 level of significance.

Users had significantly higher rates of membership in fishing organizations than non-users.

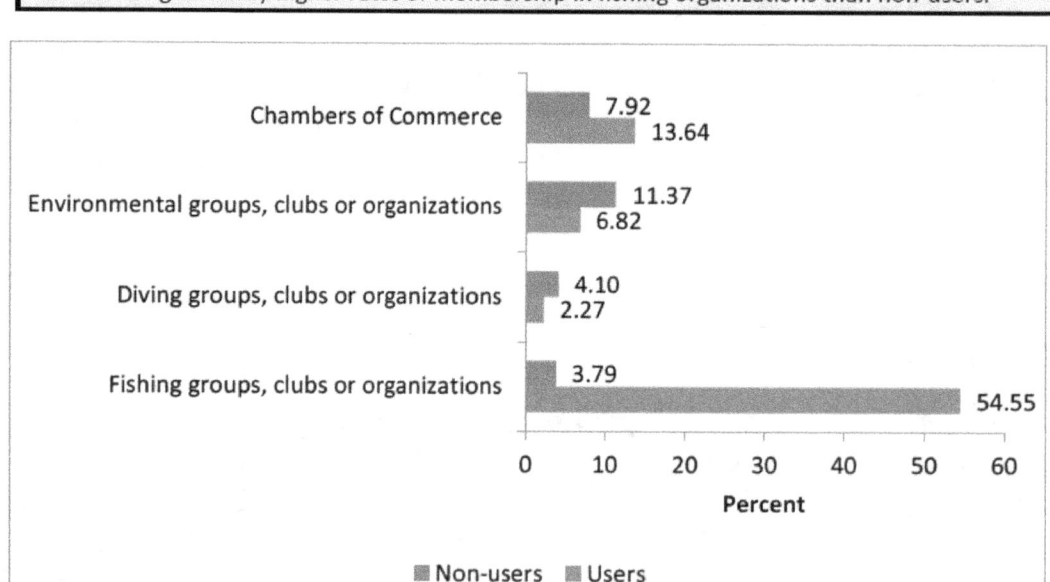

Figure 3.9 *User's versus Non-users Memberships in Groups, Clubs and Organizations: Version 2 Surveys*

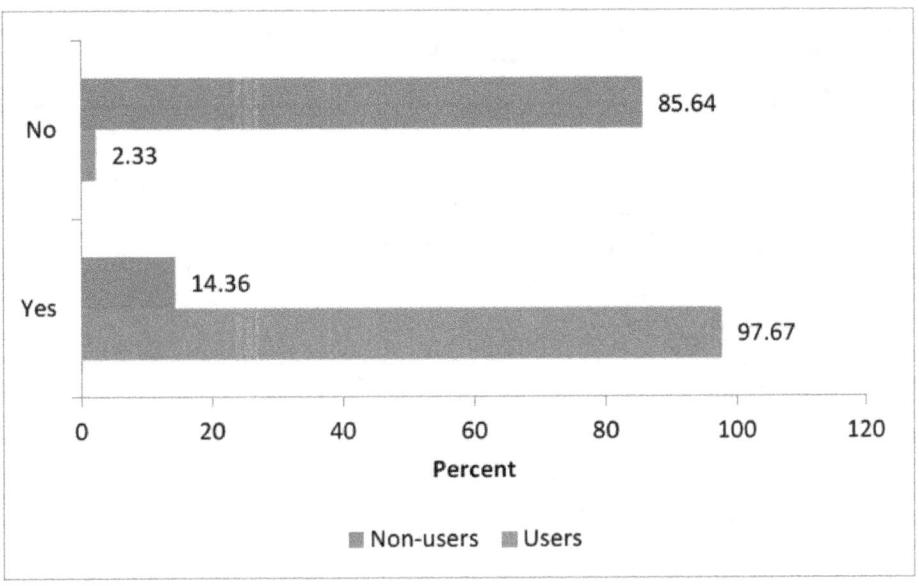

Figure 3.10 *Boat Ownership of Users versus Non-users of GRNMS: Version 2 Surveys*

Activity Participation and Use

For activities known to occur in GRNMS, users had higher rates of participation in the coastal and ocean waters off the coast of Georgia for consumptive activities, especially fishing, than non-users. Non-users had significantly higher participation rates in nonconsumptive activities, but the differences were not statistically significant (Figure 3.11). For selected activities that would not occur in GRNMS, the only statistically significant difference between users and non-users was for participation in "Beach activities" in favor of users (Figure 3.12). Use was measured in person-days where a person-day is equal to one person doing an activity for a whole day or any part of a day. Use was summarized as annual mean number of person-days by activity. Activities included were limited to the activities that are known to occur in GRNMS and are reported in two sets of means: "All Users and Non-users", which includes those who did zero person-days and "Participants Only", which includes only those who did at least one person-day of activity. For activities with low participation rates, sample sizes for the "Participants Only" sample were not large enough to support statistical tests for differences. The results are summarized in Table 3.4.

For selected activities that would not occur in GRNMS, the only statistically significant difference between users and non-users was for participation in beach activities.

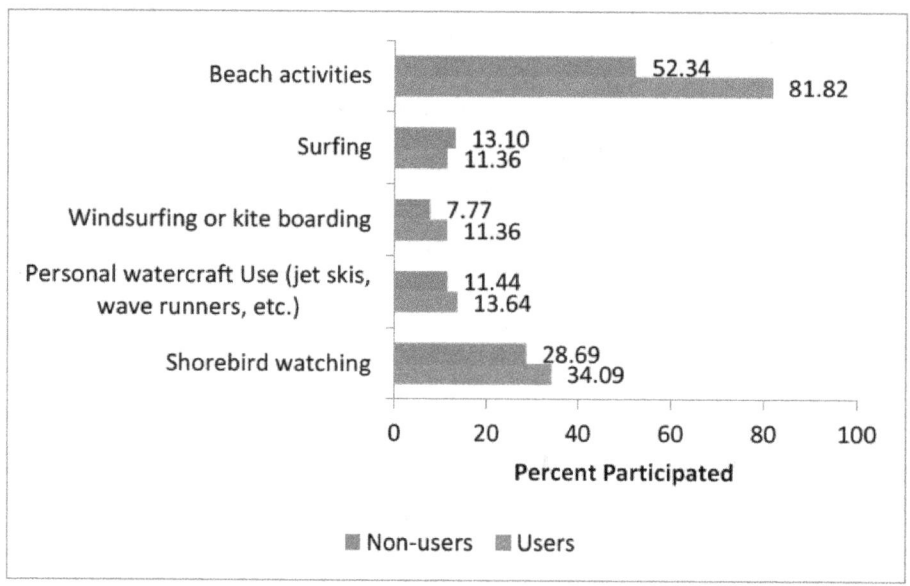

Figure 3.11 *User's versus Non-user's Activity Participation in GA: Version 2 Surveys*

For activities known to occur in GRNMS, users had higher rates of participation in Georgia's coastal and ocean waters for consumptive activities, especially fishing, than non-users. Non-users had higher participation rates in nonconsumptive activities, but the differences were not statistically significant.

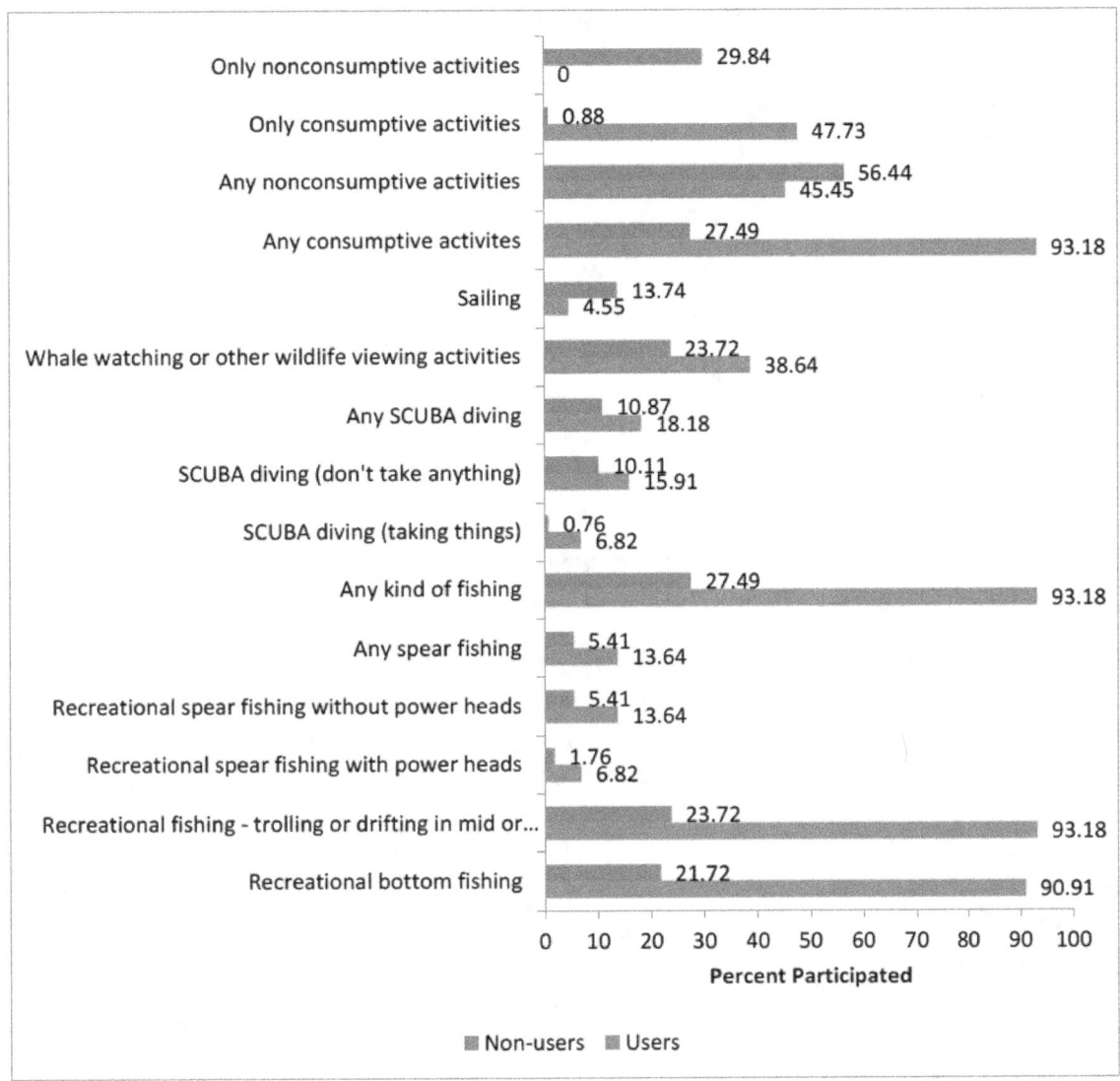

Figure 3.12 *User's versus Non-users Activity Participation in GA for Selected Activities: Version 2 Surveys*

Table 3.4. Days of Participation in Selected Activities in GA, Users versus Non-users of GRNMS: Version 2 Surveys

Activity	All Users & Non Users[1]			Participants Only[2]		
	Users (Mean)	Non-users (Mean)	Statistically Significant Difference[3]	Users (Mean)	Non-users (Mean)	Statistically Significant Difference[3]
Recreational bottom fishing	29.14	2.77	Yes	32.13	15.05	No
Recreational fishing - trolling or drfting in mid or top water	21.95	2.98	Yes	23.64	14.15	No
Recreational spear fishing with power heads	0.09	0.22	No	*	*	*
Recreational spear fishing without power heads	0.22	0.40	No	*	*	*
SCUBA diving (taking things)	0.14	0.00	No	*	*	*
SCUBA diving (don't take anything)	0.52	0.89	No	*	*	*
Whale Watching or other wildlife viewing activities	2.20	2.26	No	6.77	9.15	No

1. Includes those who did zero days of activity.
2. Includes only those that did at least one day of activity.
3. Yes means statistically significant using a t-test at .05 level of significance.
* sample size too small

<u>All Users and Non-users</u> - Users had higher average annual number of person-days of use for "recreational bottom fishing" (29.14 person-days for users and 2.77 person-days for non-users) and recreational fishing-trolling or drifting in mid or top water (21.95 person-days for users and 2.98 person-days for non-users), There were no statistically significant differences for other activities.

<u>Participants Only</u> - Sample sizes only supported estimation of means to support statistical tests for three of the seven activities for this sub-sample of users and non-users. There were no statistically significant differences.

Concern about the Health of Coastal and Ocean Areas

The survey asked respondents about their level of concern on 14 issues regarding the health of ocean and coastal areas. Respondents were first asked about their level of concern for these 14 issues in the coastal and ocean waters in and around Georgia outside GRNMS, then about them inside GRNMS. A five-point Likert scale for level of concern was used with 1=Not concerned at all, 2=Not very concerned, 3=Neutral, 4=Somewhat concerned, and 5=Extremely concerned.

In and Around Georgia outside GRNMS

There were statistically significant differences between users and non-users for 12 of the 14 issues. "Mining of Minerals and "Habitat loss from coastal development" were the two issues where there wasn't a statistically significant difference between users and non-users. Both users and non-users had relatively high concern for "Habitat loss from coastal development" and a moderate concern for "Mining of minerals". Non-users were more concerned than users for the other 12 issues (Table 3.5).

In GRNMS

There were statistically significant differences between users and non-users for 13 of the 14 issues. "Mining of minerals" was the only issue where there wasn't a statistically significant difference. Again, both users and non-users were only moderately concerned with "Mining of minerals". As with the concerns outside GRNMS, non-users of GRNMS were more concerned with all the other issues inside GRNMS than users (Table 3.6).

Table 3 5   Concern about the Health of Coastal & Ocean Areas in and around Georgia Outside of GRNMS: Users vs Non-users Version 2 Surveys

Issue	User Group	No Concerned at all	Not Very Concerned	Neutral	Somewhat Concerned	Extremely Concerned	Mean	Statistically Significant Difference [1]
1 Ocean acidification	User	9 52	14 29	33 33	33 33	9 52	3 19	Yes
	Non-user	2 97	19 75	11 30	31 54	34 43	3 74	Yes
2 Climate change	User	23 81	16 67	26 19	30 95	2 38	2 71	Yes
	Non-user	7 51	5 60	18 90	13 85	54 13	4 01	Yes
3 Sea level rise	User	23 81	19 05	26 19	28 57	2 38	2 67	Yes
	Non-user	5 88	7 89	18 50	13 79	53 94	4 02	Yes
4 Over fishing (catching more than can be replaced)	User	19 51	9 76	14 63	29 27	26 83	3 34	Yes
	Non-user	3 61	14 86	5 68	28 67	47 19	4 01	Yes
5 Coral reef health or other live bottom habitat	User	4 76	7 14	14 29	38 10	35 71	3 93	Yes
	Non-user	4 04	4 16	1 08	40 35	50 38	4 29	No
6 Marine animal's health	User	7 14	4 76	16 67	52 38	19 05	3 71	Yes
	Non-user	1 77	2 27	4 40	36 68	54 88	4 41	Yes
7 Shipping (marine transportation)	User	11 90	21 43	30 95	23 81	11 90	3 02	Yes
	Non-user	2 20	5 17	42 79	40 24	9 59	3 50	Yes
8 Dredging/Offshore dredge disposal	User	7 14	19 05	19 05	35 71	19 05	3 40	Yes
	Non-user	3 31	6 73	15 12	28 74	46 10	4 08	Yes
9 Beach renourishment	User	7 14	19 05	35 71	28 57	9 52	3 14	Yes
	Non-user	1 89	5 47	20 49	46 79	25 35	3 88	Yes
10 Energy production (oil & gas)	User	23 81	21 43	21 43	16 67	16 67	2 81	Yes
	Non-user	4 93	2 68	5 91	24 90	61 58	4 36	Yes
11 Alternative energy production (wind, tidal, and wave)	User	21 43	23 81	28 57	19 05	7 14	2 67	Yes
	Non-user	5 57	4 31	22 71	20 38	47 03	3 99	Yes

1 Top Yes/No is the test of the difference in distributions of scores using the Chi-square and Jonckheere-Terpstra (JT) tests at the 0 05
   level of significance A Yes/No means the Chi-square test was significant but the JT test was not The lower Yes/No is the test of the
   mean scores using a t-test at 0 05 level of significance

Table 3 5   Concern about the Health of Coastal & Ocean Areas in and around Georgia Outside of GRNMS: Users vs Non-users (continued)

Issue	User Group	No Concerned at all	Not Very Concerned	Neutral	Somewhat Concerned	Extremely Concerned	Mean	Statistically Significant Difference [1]
12 Mining of minerals (including sand)	User	11 90	21 43	16 67	28 57	21 43	3 26	Yes/No
	Non-user	4 48	7 26	52 28	19 98	16 00	3 36	No
13 Habitat loss from coastal development	User	2 38	16 67	4 76	40 48	35 71	3 90	Yes/No
	Non-user	0 69	1 09	7 71	48 49	42 01	4 30	No
14 Pollution (contaminants such as mercury, PCBs, sewage, pesticides)	User	2 38	2 38	11 90	28 57	54 76	4 31	Yes
	Non-user	0 69	1 08	1 08	22 36	74 79	4 69	Yes

1   Top Yes/No is the test of the difference in distributions of scores using the Chi-square and Jonckheere-Terpstra (JT) tests at the 0 05

level of significance   A Yes/No means the Chi-square test was significant but the JT test was not   The lower Yes/No is the test of the

mean scores using a t-test at 0 05 level of significance

Table 3 6   Concern about the Health of Coastal & Ocean Areas inside GRNMS: Users vs Non-users Version 2 Surveys

Issue	User Group	No Concerned at all	Not Very Concerned	Neutral	Somewhat Concerned	Extremely Concerned	Mean	Statistically Significant Difference [1]
1 Ocean acidification	User	11 90	9 52	30 95	33 33	14 29	3 29	Yes
	Non-user	4 13	19 27	5 93	30 19	40 48	3 84	Yes
2 Climate change	User	24 39	14 63	26 83	26 83	7 32	2 78	Yes
	Non-user	7 25	5 70	18 03	11 53	57 48	4 06	Yes
3 Sea level rise	User	26 19	19 05	28 57	21 43	4 76	2 59	Yes
	Non-user	6 44	8 04	22 03	7 04	56 45	3 99	Yes
4 Over fishing (catching more than can be replaced)	User	28 57	7 14	14 29	28 57	21 43	3 07	Yes
	Non-user	1 77	3 64	6 85	39 78	47 96	4 29	Yes
5 Coral reef health or other live bottom habitat	User	4 76	7 14	11 90	42 86	33 33	3 93	Yes
	Non-user	3 28	3 64	16 90	16 60	59 59	4 26	No
6 Marine animal's health	User	4 76	7 14	26 19	42 86	19 05	3 64	Yes
	Non-user	1 77	4 39	17 66	21 30	54 88	4 23	Yes
7 Shipping (marine transportation)	User	7 14	21 43	38 10	19 05	14 29	3 12	Yes
	Non-user	1 45	4 09	36 71	43 88	13 88	3 65	Yes
8 Dredging/Offshore dredge disposal	User	4 65	18 60	16 28	32 56	27 91	3 60	Yes
	Non-user	2 96	5 17	12 22	33 30	46 36	4 15	Yes
9 Beach renourishment	User	9 30	18 60	34 88	23 26	13 95	3 14	Yes
	Non-user	1 89	4 84	13 95	50 25	29 06	4 00	Yes
10 Energy production (oil & gas)	User	23 26	23 26	18 60	11 63	23 26	2 88	Yes
	Non-user	4 18	0 76	6 35	25 56	63 15	4 43	Yes
11 Alternative energy production (wind, tidal, and wave)	User	20 93	25 58	30 23	11 63	11 63	2 67	Yes
	Non-user	3 72	5 32	8 53	31 50	50 94	4 21	Yes

1 Top Yes/No is the test of the difference in distributions of scores using the Chi-square and Jonckheere-Terpstra (JT) tests at the 0 05
     level of significance   A Yes/No means the Chi-square test was significant but the JT test was not   The lower Yes/No is the test of the
     mean scores using a t-test at 0 05 level of significance

Table 3 6   Concern about the Health of Coastal & Ocean Areas inside GRNMS: Users vs Non-users (continued)

Issue	User Group	No Concerned at all	Not Very Concerned	Neutral	Somewhat Concerned	Extremely Concerned	Mean	Statistically Significant Difference [1]
12 Mining of minerals (including sand)	User	13 95	18 60	16 28	23 26	27 91	3 33	No
	Non-user	2 66	4 91	51 13	20 26	21 05	3 52	No
13 Habitat loss from coastal development	User	2 33	16 28	18 60	30 23	32 56	3 74	Yes
	Non-user	0 69	1 08	20 26	25 90	52 07	4 28	Yes
14 Pollution (contaminants such as mercury, PCBs, sewage, pesticides)	User	0 00	4 65	13 95	32 56	48 84	4 26	Yes
	Non-user	0 69	1 08	3 35	14 17	80 71	4 73	Yes

1 Top Yes/No is the test of the difference in distributions of scores using the Chi-square and Jonckheere-Terpstra (JT) tests at the 0 05

   level of significance   A Yes/No means the Chi-square test was significant but the JT test was not   The lower Yes/No is the test of the

   mean scores using a t-test at 0 05 level of significance

Ways Users and Non-users of GRNMS Value Coastal and Ocean Resources/Marine Environment

The survey asked respondents for their level of value for 10 uses of coastal and ocean resources. The level of value used was a five-point Likert scale where 1=No value, 2=Low value, 3=Medium value, 4=High value, and 5=Extremely high value. Non-users had higher values for all 10 of the uses of GRNMS than users except for "Support for recreation activities". The differences in levels of values between users and non-users were statistically significant for all 10 uses (Table 3.7).

Table 3 7 Ways Users versus Non-users of GRNMS Value Coastal & Ocean Resources/Marine Environment Version 2 Surveys

Good or Service	User Group	No Value	Low Value	Medium Value	High Value	Extremely High Value	Mean	Statistically Significant Difference [1]
a Support for recreation activities	User	2 38	2 38	9 52	45 24	40 48	4 19	Yes
	Non-user	2 99	1 92	33 27	41 66	20 16	3 74	Yes
b Seafood purchased at local stores and restaurants	User	4 65	18 60	27 91	25 58	23 26	3 44	Yes
	Non-user	3 75	1 08	8 33	40 28	46 56	4 25	Yes
c Seafood purchased at non local stores & restaurants	User	26 19	26 19	35 71	7 14	4 76	2 38	Yes
	Non-user	4 58	16 40	35 64	32 73	10 65	3 28	Yes
d Support for Scientific Research	User	6 82	9 09	40 91	27 27	15 91	3 36	Yes
	Non-user	1 45	15 93	17 05	25 92	39 65	3 86	Yes
e Support for education	User	6 82	2 27	31 82	34 09	25 00	3 68	Yes
	Non-user	1 45	2 92	12 30	17 90	65 43	4 43	Yes
f Supply of mineral resources through mining	User	29 55	27 27	34 09	6 82	2 27	2 25	Yes
	Non-user	2 50	29 71	26 63	32 81	8 34	3 14	Yes
g Supply of oil & gas	User	16 28	9 30	34 88	13 95	25 58	3 23	Yes
	Non-user	5 87	9 44	16 27	20 62	47 79	3 95	Yes
h Supply of alternative energy (wind, wave, tidal)	User	15 91	13 64	36 36	18 18	15 91	3 04	Yes
	Non-user	2 53	18 72	12 64	22 56	43 54	3 86	Yes
i Supply of pharmaceutical products through mining or harvest of resources	User	20 45	27 27	25 00	18 18	9 09	2 68	Yes
	Non-user	1 45	22 66	15 07	42 97	17 85	3 53	Yes
j Protection of resources even though I never intend to visit or directly use them	User	11 36	11 36	34 09	25 00	18 18	3 27	Yes
	Non-user	1 45	14 10	8 65	22 54	53 27	4 12	Yes

1 Top Yes/No is the test of the difference in distributions of scores using the Chi-square and Jonckheere-Terpstra (JT) tests at the 0 05

   level of significance   A Yes/No means the Chi-square test was significant but the JT test was not   The lower Yes/No is the test of the

   mean scores using a t-test at 0 05 level of significance

Actions Users and Non-users of GRNMS would take to ensure Sustainability of Coastal and Ocean Resources

The survey asked respondents about the activities or actions they would take to ensure that coastal and ocean resources are used sustainably and available for future generations. Nine activities or actions were presented and a five-point Likert scale was used to score to what extent respondents would undertake each activity or action, where 1=Would not do, 2=Would do very little, 3=Would do some, 4=Would do a lot, and 5=Would do the maximum.

For "Volunteering time", a majority of both users and non-users would do some to would do the maximum with 67.5% for users and 55.5% for non-users. For "Paying higher taxes for resource protection and restoration", a majority of both users and non-users would not do or would do very little with 72% for users and about 60% for non-users (Table 3.8).

Table 3 8   Activities or Actions Users versus Non-users of GRNMS Would Do to ensure that coastal and ocean resources are used sustainably and available for future generations to enjoy Version 2 Surveys

Activity or Action	User Group	Would Not Do	Would do Very Little	Would Do Some	Would Do a Lot	Would do the Maximum	Mean	Statistically Significant Difference [1]
a Volunter time	User	7 50	25 00	50 00	15 00	2 50	2 80	No
	Non-user	10 50	34 10	45 41	4 42	5 57	2 60	No
b Pay higher taxes for resource protection and restoration	User	46 51	25 58	20 93	2 33	4 65	1 93	Yes
	Non-user	23 12	31 76	36 30	7 23	1 58	2 32	No
c Pay higher prices for goods and services due to costs to businesses in complying with regulations that protect ocean & coastal resources or require restoration of areas damaged	User	31 82	25 00	25 00	6 82	11 36	2 41	Yes
	Non-user	3 76	15 20	58 65	14 80	7 59	3 07	Yes
d Pay user fees like fishing licenses or diving access fees or additional boat registration fees	User	38 64	27 27	27 27	4 55	2 27	2 04	Yes
	Non-user	13 46	22 01	48 44	16 09	0 00	2 67	Yes
e Donate to groups respresenting recreational fishing interests	User	11 63	9 30	51 16	20 93	6 98	3 02	Yes
	Non-user	21 39	31 97	42 92	2 96	0 76	2 30	Yes
f Donate to groups representing diving interests	User	42 86	19 05	26 19	9 52	2 38	2 09	No
	Non-user	45 81	11 83	38 64	2 96	0 76	2 01	No
g Recycle	User	4 65	6 98	32 56	32 56	23 26	3 63	Yes
	Non-user	1 89	2 38	20 78	21 06	53 88	4 23	Yes
h Use less energy	User	6 98	16 28	41 86	16 28	18 60	3 23	Yes
	Non-user	1 89	3 36	29 91	21 13	43 71	4 01	Yes
i Avoid/boycott certain seafood products	User	25 00	15 91	29 55	11 36	18 18	2 82	No
	Non-user	21 37	6 68	39 02	9 34	23 59	3 07	No

1   Top Yes/No is the test of the difference in distributions of scores using the Chi-square and Jonckheere-Terpstra (JT) tests at the 0 05 level of significance   A Yes/No means the Chi-square test was significant but the JT test was not   The lower Yes/No is the test of the mean scores using a t-test at 0 05 level of significance

A majority of users (56.82%) would not do or would do very little in "paying higher prices as a result of regulations", while a majority of non-users (58.65%) were neutral on this issue. A majority of users were also opposed to paying higher user fees as about 66% would not do or would do very little, while about 19% of non-users would not do or do very little (Table 3.8).

User fees are a complicated issue and often elicit emotional responses. The literature on user fees supports the notion that people are willing to pay user fees for the activities that they participate in (Aukerman 1987, Brown 1992, Fedler and Miles 1989, Kyle et al 2002, Leeworthy 1993, and Winter et al 1999). They do not want to subsidize the activities of others. If general taxes are used to pay to support recreational or other activities or goods and services they don't consume, they generally do not support them. This is what is being picked up by the response to "pay higher taxes for resource protection and restoration". One can see this more clearly by looking at the response to "pay higher prices for goods and services due to costs to businesses in complying with regulations that protect ocean & coastal resources or require restoration of areas damaged". In this case, people are paying only for the goods and services they consume through the prices that are passed onto them by suppliers. What is interesting in the current findings is that a majority of users are against all forms of paying for protection and/or restoration of ocean & coastal resources. Non-users are generally more supportive than users for the use of prices and user fees for paying for protection and/or restoration of ocean and coastal resources.

The differences in willingness to donate to groups representing recreational fishing interests correlates with users participation rates in recreational fishing with users willing to donate more than non-users with 79% of users willing do some to the maximum, while only about 47% of non-users are willing to do the same (Table 3.8). This correlation between activity participation also shows up in the willingness to donate to groups representing diving interests. Both users and non-users have low participation rates in diving and a majority of both users and non-users would not do or do very little with about 62% for users and about 58% for non-users.

A majority of both users and non-users would do some to doing the maximum for recycling with non-users willing to do significantly more. More than 88% of users would do some to do the maximum, while about 96% of non-users would do some to do the maximum.

A majority of both users and non-users would also be willing to use less energy with non-users willing to do more than users. About 77% of users would do some to do the maximum, while about 95% of non-users would do some to do the maximum.

A majority of both users and non-users were willing to avoid or boycott certain seafood products, but the differences were not significantly different. More than 59% of users would do some to would do the maximum in avoiding or boycotting certain seafood products, while about 72% of non-users would do some to would do the maximum in avoiding or boycotting certain seafood products.

Support for Protection of Coastal and Ocean Resources

The survey asked respondents about their level of support for protection of resources outside and inside GRNMS; support for marine reserves outside and inside GRNMS; support for research only areas outside and inside GRNMS; support for multi-species fishery management: and support for ecosystem-based management. A five-point Likert scale for support was used with 1=No support at all, 2=Somewhat against, 3=Neutral, 4=Somewhat support and 5=Strongly support. Support for the use of marine zoning was a simple yes or no response.

Support for Protection of Resources Outside and Inside GRNMS

Non-users showed significantly more support for protection of resources both outside and inside GRNMS. More than 94% of non-users either strongly or somewhat supported protection outside GRNMS, while about 55% of users either strongly or somewhat supported protection outside GRNMS. Similarly, about 89% of non-users either strongly or somewhat supported protections inside GRNMS, while about 63% of users either strongly or somewhat supported protections inside GRNMS (Table 3.9).

Table 3 9 Comparisons of Users and Non-users of GRNMS on Support for Various Coastal & Ocean Resource Protection Strategies Version 2 Surveys

Statement	User Group	No Support at All	Somewhat Against	Neutral	Somewhat Support	Strongly Support	Mean	Statistically Significant Difference1
1 Support for Protection of Coastal & Ocean Resources								
a Protection Outside GRNMS	User	9 52	28 57	7 14	33 33	21 43	3 29	Yes
	Non-user	0 69	1 08	3 21	60 35	34 66	4 27	Yes
b Protection Inside GRNMS	User	11 63	16 28	9 3	37 21	25 58	3 49	Yes
	Non-user	0 69	1 08	9 42	26 68	62 13	4 49	Yes
2 Support for Marine Reserves								
a In GA Outside GRNMS	User	73 81	4 76	2 38	14 29	4 76	1 71	Yes
	Non-user	5 96	7 80	4 35	26 03	55 85	4 18	Yes
b Inside GRNMS	User	69 05	9 52	4 76	11 9	4 76	1 88	Yes
	Non-user	4 99	2 50	11 77	27 11	53 63	4 45	Yes
3 Support for Research Only Areas								
a In GA Outside GRNMS	User	70 73	7 32	7 32	4 88	9 76	1 76	Yes
	Non-user	6 95	0 57	12 09	69 36	11 02	3 77	Yes
b Inside GRNMS	User	69 05	9 52	4 76	11 90	4 76	1 74	Yes
	Non-user	4 99	2 50	11 77	27 11	53 63	4 22	Yes
3 Support for Multi-species Management	User	27 27	11 36	27 27	27 27	6 82	2 75	Yes
	Non-user	0 69	6 93	52 86	14 07	25 45	3 57	Yes
4 Support for Ecosystem-based Management	User	38 64	15 91	25 00	13 64	6 82	2 34	Yes
	Non-user	2 98	1 52	26 44	44 95	24 11	3 86	Yes

1 Top Yes/No is the test of the difference in distributions of scores using the Chi-square and Jonckheere-Terpstra (JT) tests at the 0 05 level of

significance A Yes/No means the Chi-square test was significant but the JT test was not The lower Yes/No is the test of the mean scores

using a t-test at 0 05 level of significance

Support for Marine Zoning

Non-users were much more supportive of the use of marine zoning in the ocean and coastal areas off the coast of Georgia than users. Non-users overwhelmingly supported the approach with about 76% responding yes, while users were overwhelmingly against with more than 60% responding no (Figure 3.13).

Non-users were much more supportive of the use of marine zoning off the coast of Georgia than users.

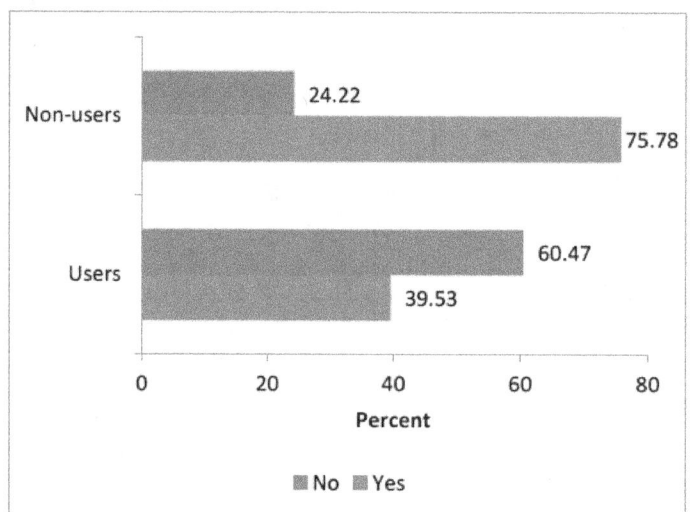

Figure 3.13 *Users versus Non-users Support for Use of Marine Zoning of Georgia*

Support for Marine Reserves

Marine reserves area special type of marine zoning in which nothing is allowed to be taken, so they are also known as no-take areas. Non-users were much more supportive of the use of marine reserves both outside and inside GRNMS than users. About 82% of non-users either strongly or somewhat supported marine reserves outside GRNMS and about 81% either strongly or somewhat supported marine reserves inside GRNMS. In stark contrast, 78.57% of users either had no support at all or were somewhat against marine reserves both outside and inside GRNMS (Table 3.9).

A follow-up question was asked of respondents about how much impact was acceptable on nine different user groups that would be displaced from using GRNMS if marine reserves were implemented. Impacts were measured in percent of a group's activity. Non-users would accept higher impacts on all nine groups than users. The differences were statistically significant for seven of the nine user groups (Table 3.10).

68

Table 3.10 *Maximum Acceptable Percent Impact on Various Activities from Marine Reserves in GRNMS: Users versus Non-users Version 2 Surveys*

Activity	User Group	Mean	Statististically Significant Difference [1]
Recreational bottom fishing	User	25.71	No
	Non-user	37.04	
Recreational fishing - trolling or drifting in mid or top water	User	22.50	Yes
	Non-user	54.99	
Recreational spear fishing without power heads	User	14.40	Yes
	Non-user	49.87	
Recreational spear fishing with power heads	User	40.71	No
	Non-user	50.05	
Commercial bottom fishing	User	13.10	Yes
	Non-user	37.95	
Commercial fishing - trolling or drifting mid or top water	User	13.69	Yes
	Non-user	36.88	
Commercial spear fishing with power heads	User	12.38	Yes
	Non-user	38.87	
Commercial spear fishing without power heads	User	12.38	Yes
	Non-user	40.24	
SCUBA diving (taking things)	User	13.81	Yes
	Non-user	38.50	

1. The test is a t-test of the mean score at the 0.05 level of significance.

Support for Research Only Areas

Research Only Areas are a more restrictive form of zoning than marine reserves because they displace all uses except science and education. As with all zoning strategies, non-users were much more supportive of the use of research only areas both outside and inside GRNMS than users. More than 80% of non-users either strongly or somewhat supported both the use of research only areas outside and inside GRNMS. Again in stark contrast, more than 78% of users either had no support at all or were somewhat against the use of research only areas both outside and inside GRNMS (Table 3.9).

A follow-up question was asked of respondents about how much impact was acceptable on nine different user groups that would be displaced from using GRNMS if research only areas were implemented. Impacts were measured in percent of a group's activity. Non-users would accept higher impacts on all nine groups than users. The differences were statistically significant for only one user group (SCUBA Diving – taking things) (Table 3.11).

Table 3.11 *Maximum Acceptable Percent Impact on Various Activities from Research Only Areas in GRNMS: Users versus Non-users Version 2 Surveys*

Activity	User Group	Mean	Statististically Significant Difference [1]
Recreational bottom fishing	User	23.90	No
	Non-user	34.14	
Recreational fishing - trolling or drifting in mid or top water	User	22.62	No
	Non-user	32.92	
Recreational spear fishing without power heads	User	16.31	No
	Non-user	30.79	
Recreational spear fishing with power heads	User	18.81	No
	Non-user	28.92	
Commercial bottom fishing	User	16.79	No
	Non-user	28.02	
Commercial fishing - trolling or drifting mid or top water	User	16.79	No
	Non-user	26.78	
Commercial spear fishing with power heads	User	16.07	No
	Non-user	24.14	
Commercial spear fishing without power heads	User	16.07	No
	Non-user	20.86	
SCUBA diving (taking things)	User	16.07	Yes
	Non-user	32.44	

1. The test is a t-test of the mean score at the 0.05 level of significance.

Support for Multi-species Fishery Management

Respondents to the survey were presented with an alternative approach to the currently used approach that manages fisheries on a species-by-species basis. They were told that the multi-species approach looks at various inter-relationships between species such as predator-prey relationships (big fish eat little fish). Non-users were more supportive of this approach to fishery management than users. But neither group had a majority supporting this approach. A majority of non-users were neutral (52.86%) and a plurality (38.63%) of users either had no support at all or were somewhat against this approach. More than 39% of non-users either strongly or somewhat supported this approach, while 34% of users either strongly or somewhat supported this approach (Table 3.9).

Support for Ecosystem-based Management

Respondents to the survey were also presented with an alternative approach to management called ecosystem-based management. In this approach respondents were told that this approach recognizes all human uses and values and attempts to achieve a balance across many uses and values. Again, non-users were more supportive of this approach than users. About 60% of non-users either strongly or somewhat supported this approach, while only about 20% of users either strongly or somewhat supported this approach. A majority of users (54.55%) either had no support at all or were somewhat against this approach (Table 3.9).

Discussion

In this report, results of version 2 of a survey of users of GRNMS are reported on their attitudes on several policy/management strategies both inside and outside GRNMS in the coastal and ocean waters off the Georgia coast. Questions were asked about marine zoning in general and specific forms of marine zoning (e.g. no-take marine reserves, which allow non-consumptive activities and research only areas, which prohibit all consumptive and non-consumptive activities, except research and education). Users were also asked about fishery management options such as multispecies management and ecosystem-based management.

The findings were that a majority of GRNMS users were against all of these policy/management strategies both inside and outside GRNMS in coastal and ocean waters off the coast of Georgia, and this was contrasted with non-users of GRNMS (general Georgia population), of which a majority supported all the policy/management options addressed.

With respect to marine zoning, and especially marine reserves or no-take areas, these findings are contrary to some of the findings elsewhere. Leeworthy (2006) found that a majority of recreational reef users in southeast Florida and the Florida Keys National Marine Sanctuary (FKNMS) supported no-take areas. This continued to be true when users were segmented into three groups: 1) Fish Only, 2) Fish & Dive and 3) Dive Only. Although a majority of all three groups supported the no-take areas, the percent support declined the more consumptive the activity group. Loper (2008) conducted similar tests for users of the Channel Islands National Marine Sanctuary (CINMS) who accessed the sanctuary via private household boats for recreation. A similar pattern to that found in Florida was found as the more consumptive the activities participated in, the lower the support for no-take areas. In this case, a majority of those who fish only did not support the no-take areas.

The users of GRNMS are mostly engaged in consumptive activities with 95% engaged in fishing, with few engaged in non-consumptive activities. In the case of the southeast Florida and the FKNMS and the CINMS, a large proportion of users did both consumptive and non-consumptive activities, so they have an appreciation for having sites set aside so they can have a quality experience for all their activities. So given the low proportion of users of GRNMS that also do non-consumptive activities, it is not surprising that a majority of GRNMS users are against any marine zoning alternatives that displace consumptive uses.

There is also a time dimension and learning that can change users' attitudes. In the FKNMS, three user groups were studied and measurements compared over a decadal period. The three groups were commercial fishers (the most consumptive group), dive shop owners/operators (modest consumptive use) and members of local environmental groups (least consumptive group). The baseline measurements on attitudes about no-take areas were taken in 1995-96 and were reported in Milon et al (1997) and Suman et al (1999). Repeat measurements were taken in 2004-05 for commercial fishermen and dive shop owners operators and 2007 for members of local environmental groups and were reported in Shivlani et al (2008). In Shivlani et al (2008), tests were done for statistically significant changes in attitudes. In the baseline, commercial fishers were highly non-supportive with an overwhelming majority against no-take areas. After almost a decade of implementation of no-take areas, the opposition has declined significantly; however, a majority still don't support no-take areas. A majority of dive shop owners/operators was supportive of the no-take areas in both the baseline and the decadal replication. However, over the period of the baseline study there were outside influences that warned stakeholder groups that the no-take areas established in the FKNMS were part of a larger "federal takeover" and that eventually all uses would be displaced from all areas. So in the baseline, although a majority supported the no-take areas, it was a slim majority. After almost a decade of implementation, an overwhelming majority of dive shop owners and operators support the no-take areas. The point here is that the attitudes expressed by GRNMS users are a baseline estimate when the current "research only area" has only been implemented for a short time. The fears generated by several organizations lobbying against loss of access via no-take areas most likely have had great influence on the predominantly consumptive users of GRNMS. We might expect that with more time to experience what actually happens to the conditions of GRNMS, this attitude could change with a movement towards more support.

A portion of the data collected from users of GRNMS has not yet been analyzed. The portion consists of the questions that support "Specialization Theory". Specialization theory is a way to

72

classify users into categories with predictive powers. Specialization theory was first proposed by Bryan (1977) and re-conceptualized for hypothesis testing by Ditton et al (1992). One of the basic propositions of "Specialization theory" is that more specialized users will be more supportive of rules and regulations impacting their use, especially if there are expected long-term benefits from the rules and regulations. Salz and Loomis (2005) tested specialization theory for saltwater sports fishers in the northeast US on their support for no-take marine protected areas. They found no difference across specialization efforts, which was contrary to specialization theory with a majority of this user group opposed to no-take marine protected areas. This was a baseline assessment where no-take areas were not yet in existence, so users had not yet experienced the actual impacts of the no-take areas. As Salz et al (2005) noted "users' attitudes will be determined by the balancing of loss of access versus whether there are net benefits via possible 'replenishment effects' often hypothesized from no-take areas".

Future Research

In future research, specialization theory could be tested using the data on GRNMS users. In addition, data from all visitor and recreational users was obtained in a 2007-08 survey of users of the FKNMS (Leeworthy et al 2010 and Leeworthy and Morris 2010). The specialization theory questions were also asked in the Florida Keys surveys. Given the differences in the diversity of activity participation between users of GRNMS and users of the FKNMS, testing specialization theory in both sanctuaries about no-take areas could yield important insights.

Also given that users can change their attitudes over time, as they experience what actually happens post implementation of no-take marine reserves or research only areas, the surveys of GRNMS users should be replicated in approximately 10 years to test for any changes.

REFERENCES

Aukerman, Robert. 1987. User Pays for Recreation Resources. Fort Collins, Colorado: Colorado State University, Research Services.

Bishop, Richard C., David J. Chapman, Barbara J. Kanninen, Jon A. Krosnick, Bob Leeworthy, and Norman F. Meade. 2001. Total Economic Value for Protecting and Restoring Hawaiian Coral Reef Ecosystems: Final Report. Silver Spring, MD: NOAA Office of National Marine Sanctuaries, Office of Response and Restoration, and Coral Reef Conservation Program. NOAA Technical Memorandum CRCP 16.406 pp. Available at http://coralreef.noaa.gov/aboutcrcp/news/featuredstories/oct11/hi_value/resources/protecting_res toring_hawaiian_cre.pdf

Brown, LaTonya L. 1992. A Legislative History of Outdoor Recreation User Fees. Congressional Research Service, Library of Congress, Washington, D.C. August 14, 1992, 23pp.

Bryan, H. 1977. Leisure Value Systems and Recreational Specialization: the Case of Trout Fishermen. *Journal of Leisure Research*, 9, 174-187.

Dillman, D. A.. 1978. Mail and Telephone Surveys: The Total Design Method. Wiley-Interscience, New York, NY.

Ditton, Robert B., David K. Loomis, and Seungdam Choi. 1992. Recreation Specialization from a Social Worlds Perspective. *Journal of Leisure Research,* Vol. 24, No. 1, pp.33-51.

Fedler, A. J. & Miles, A. F. (1989). Paying for backcountry recreation: Understanding the acceptability of use fees. *Journal of Park and Recreation Administration,* 7 (2), 35-46.

INFO USA. Mail Survey Database for Georgia Households. 5711 S. Circle, Omaha, NE 68127.

Kyle, G., Graefe, A. & Absher, J. (2002). Determining appropriate prices for recreation on public lands. *Journal of Park and Recreation Administration, 20*(2), 69-89.

LaFranchi, Chris and Linwood Pendleton. 2008. Private Boating and Boater Activities in the Channel Islands: A spatial analysis and assessment. Final Report prepared for the Resources Legacy Fund Foundation (RLFF) and the National Marine Sanctuary Program (NMSP), March 2008, 79pp. Available at http://sanctuaries.noaa.gov/science/socioeconomic/channelislands/pdfs/privboat1.pdf

Leeworthy Vernon R. 1993. The Feasibility of User Fees in National Marine Sanctuaries: A Preliminary Characterization. Silver Spring, MD: National Oceanic and Atmospheric Administration, National Ocean Service, Strategic Environmental Assessments Division, December 1993, 24pp.

Leeworthy, Vernon R. 2006. Socioeconomic Study of Reefs in Southeast Florida, 2000-01: Resident Reef Users' Opinions on No-take Areas on Reefs. National Oceanic and Atmospheric Administration, National Ocean Service, Special Projects Office: Silver Spring, MD, May 15, 2006, pp. 9.

Leeworthy, Vernon R. 2012. Knowledge, Attitudes and Perceptions of Management Strategies and Regulations of the Gray's Reef National Marine Sanctuary by Users and Non-users of the Sanctuary. Silver Spring, MD: National Oceanic and Atmospheric Administration, Office of National Marine Sanctuaries, March 2012.
http://sanctuaries.noaa.gov/science/socioeconomic/graysreef/pdfs/grnms_kap.pdf

Leeworthy, Vernon R. 2012. Technical Appendix: Knowledge, Attitudes and Perceptions of Management Strategies and Regulations of the Gray's Reef National Marine Sanctuary by Users and Non-users of the Sanctuary. Silver Spring, MD: National Oceanic and Atmospheric Administration, Office of National Marine Sanctuaries, February 2012.
http://sanctuaries.noaa.gov/science/socioeconomic/graysreef/pdfs/grnms_kap_tech.pdf

Leeworthy, Vernon R. 2013. Technical Appendix: Knowledge, Attitudes and Perceptions of Management Strategies and Regulations of the Gray's Reef National Marine Sanctuary by Users and Non-users of the Sanctuary, Version 2. Silver Spring, MD: National Oceanic and Atmospheric Administration, Office of National Marine Sanctuaries, March 2013.

Leeworthy, Vernon R., David K. Loomis, and Shona Paterson. 2010. Visitor Profiles: Florida Keys/key West 2007-08. National Oceanic and Atmospheric Administration, National Ocean Service, Office of National marine Sanctuaries: Silver Spring, MD, June 2010, 196 pp.
http://sanctuaries.noaa.gov/science/socioeconomic/floridakeys/pdfs/full_visitor_08.pdf

Leeworthy, Vernon R. and F. Charles Morris. 2010. A Socioeconomic Analysis of the Recreation Activities of Monroe County Residents in the Florida Keys/Key West 2008. National Oceanic and Atmospheric Administration, National Ocean Service, Special Projects Office: Silver Spring, MD, September 2010, 61 pp.
http://sanctuaries.noaa.gov/science/socioeconomic/floridakeys/pdfs/floridakeysres_report.pdf

Loper, Christy. 2008. Valuing Networks of Marine Reserves: An Assessment of Recreational Users' Preferences for Marine Conservation in California's Channel Islands. PhD dissertation, Newark, DE: University of Delaware, College of Marine Studies, June 24, 2008.
Milon, J. W., D. O. Suman, M. Shivlani, and K. A. Cochran. 1997. Commercial fishers' perceptions of marine reserves for the Florida Keys National Marine Sanctuary. Florida Sea Grant Technical Paper-89.

Salz, Ronald J. and David K. Loomis. 2005. Recreation Specialization and Anglers' Attitudes Towards Restricted Fishing Areas. *Human Dimensions of Wildlife*, 10: 187-199.

Statistical Analysis System (SAS) Version 9.1. The SAS Institute, Inc. Cary, North Carolina.

Shivlani, M., Leeworthy V.R., Murray, T.J., Suman, D.O., and F. Tonioli. 2008. Knowledge, Attitudes and Perceptions of Management Strategies and Regulations of the Florida Keys National Marine Sanctuary by Commercial Fishers, Dive Operators, and Environmental Group Members: A Baseline Characterization and 10-year Comparison. Marine Sanctuaries Conservation Series ONMS-08-06. U.S. Department of Commerce, National Oceanic and Atmospheric Administration, Office of National Marine Sanctuaries, Silver Spring, MD. 170 pp. Available at http://sanctuaries.noaa.gov/science/socioeconomic/floridakeys/pdfs/kap2.pdf

Suman, D. O., M. P. Shivlani, and J. W. Milon. 1999. Perceptions and Attitudes Regarding Marine Reserves: A Comparison of Stakeholder Groups in the Florida Keys National Marine Sanctuary. Ocean and Coastal Management 42: 1019-1040.

Thomas J. Murray & Associates. 2005. Tortugas 2000-A post mortem: Evaluation of actual versus projected socioeconomic impacts of the Dry Tortugas Ecological Reserve. MARFIN final report in completion of MARFIN project NA04NMF4330079. Available at http://sanctuaries.noaa.gov/science/socioeconomic/floridakeys/pdfs/tortugasmarfin.pdf

Winter, P., Palucki, L., & Burkhardt. R. (1999). Anticipated responses to a fee program: The key is trust. *Journal of Leisure Research, 31*(3), 207-226.

www.ingramcontent.com/pod-product-compliance
Lightning Source LLC
Chambersburg PA
CBHW080423290526
45791CB00008BA/2390